Digital Technology and Contemporary Univer

Digital Technology and the Contemporary University examines the often messy realities of higher education in the 'digital age'. Drawing on a variety of theoretical and empirical perspectives, the book explores the intimate links between digital technology and wider shifts within contemporary higher education – not least the continued rise of the managerialist 'bureaucratic' university. It highlights the ways that these new trends can be challenged, and possibly changed altogether.

Addressing a persistent gap in higher education and educational technology research, where digital technology is rarely subject to an appropriately critical approach, *Digital Technology and the Contemporary University* offers an alternative reading of the social, political, economic and cultural issues surrounding universities and technology. The book highlights emerging themes that are beginning to be recognized and discussed in academia, but as yet have not been explored thoroughly. Over the course of eight wide-ranging chapters, the book addresses issues such as:

- the role of digital technology in university reform;
- digital technologies and the organization of universities;
- digital technology and the working lives of university staff;
- digital technology and the 'student experience';
- reimagining the place of digital technology within the contemporary university.

This book will be of great interest to all students, academic researchers and writers working in the areas of education studies and/or educational technology, as well as being essential reading for anyone working in the areas of higher education research and digital media research.

Neil Selwyn is Professor of Education at Monash University, Melbourne, Australia.

The Society for Research into Higher Education (SRHE) is an independent and financially self-supporting international learned Society. It is concerned to advance understanding of higher education, especially through the insights, perspectives and knowledge offered by systematic research and scholarship.

The Society's primary role is to improve the quality of higher education through facilitating knowledge exchange, discourse and publication of research. SRHE members are worldwide and the Society is an NGO in operational relations with UNESCO.

The Society has a wide set of aims and objectives. Amongst its many activities the Society:

• is a specialist publisher of higher education research, journals and books, amongst them Studies in Higher Education, Higher Education Quarterly, Research into Higher Education Abstracts and a long running monograph book series.

The Society also publishes a number of in-house guides and produces a specialist series "Issues in Postgraduate Education".

• funds and supports a large number of special interest networks for researchers and practitioners working in higher education from every discipline. These networks are open to all and offer a range of topical seminars, workshops and other events throughout the year ensuring the Society is in touch with all current research knowledge.

• runs the largest annual UK-based higher education research conference and parallel conference for postgraduate and newer researchers. This is attended by researchers from over 35 countries and showcases current research across every aspect of higher education.

SRHE *Society for Research into Higher Education*
Advancing knowledge Informing policy Enhancing practice

73 Collier Street   T +44 (0)20 7427 2350   Director: Helen Perkins
London N1 9BE   F +44 (0)20 7278 1135   Registered Charity No. 313850
United Kingdom   E srheoffice@srhe.ac.uk   Company No. 00868820
                                                       Limited by Guarantee
                          www.srhe.ac.uk   Registered office as above

Society for Research into Higher Education (SRHE) series

Series Editor: Jennifer M. Case, University of Cape Town
Jeroen Huisman, University of Ghent

Published titles:
Intellectual Leadership in Higher Education: Renewing the Role of the University Professo
Bruce Macfarlane

Strategic Curriculum Change: Global Trends in Universities
Paul Blackmore and Camille B. Kandiko

Reconstructing Identities in Higher Education: The Rise of "Third Space" Professionals
Celia Whitchurch

The University in Dissent: Scholarship in the Corporate University
Gary Rolfe

Everything for Sale? The Marketisation of UK Higher Education
Roger Brown with Helen Carasso

Literacy in the Digital University: Critical Perspectives on Learning, Scholarship and Technology
Robin Goodfellow and Mary R. Lea

Researching Student Learning in Higher Education: A Social Realist Approach
Jennifer M. Case

Women Leaders in Higher Education: Shattering the myths
Tanya Fitzgerald

Writing in Social Spaces: A social processes approach to academic writing
Rowena Murray

Digital Technology and the Contemporary University

Degrees of digitization

Neil Selwyn

LONDON AND NEW YORK

First published 2014
by Routledge
2 Park Square, Milton Park, Abingdon, Oxon OX14 4RN
together with the Society for Research into Higher Education
73 Collier Street
London N1 9BE
UK

and by Routledge
711 Third Avenue, New York, NY 10017
together with the Society for Research into Higher Education
73 Collier Street
London N1 9BE
UK

Routledge is an imprint of the Taylor & Francis Group, an informa business

© 2014 N. Selwyn

British Library Cataloguing in Publication Data
A catalogue record for this book is available from the British Library

Library of Congress Cataloging in Publication Data
Selwyn, Neil.
Digital technology and the contemporary university :
degrees of digitization / Neil Selwyn.
pages cm.—(Research into higher education)
1. Education, Higher—Computer-assisted instruction.
2. Education, Higher—Effect of technological innovations on.
3. Educational technology. 4. Digital communications. I. Title.
LB2395.7.S45 2014
378.1734—dc23
2013050555

ISBN: 978-0-415-72461-6 (hbk)
ISBN: 978-0-415-72462-3 (pbk)
ISBN: 978-1-315-76865-6 (ebk)

Typeset in Galliard
by Swales & Willis Ltd, Exeter, Devon

Contents

Series editors' introduction

This series, co-published by the Society for Research into Higher Education and Routledge Books, aims to provide, in an accessible manner, cutting-edge scholarly thinking and inquiry that reflects the rapidly changing world of higher education, examined in a global context.

Encompassing topics of wide international relevance, the series includes every aspect of the international higher education research agenda, from strategic policy formulation and impact to pragmatic advice on best practice in the field. Each book in the series aims to meet at least one of the principle aims of the Society: to advance knowledge; to enhance practice; to inform policy.

Neil Selwyn critically engages with both the future visions and contemporary realities of digital technology in higher education. With a sociological angle which emphasizes issues such as power and control, class, and commodification, he offers a unique perspective on the "politics of digital higher education". Based on a conceptually strong and empirically grounded analysis, his final conclusion points to an agenda of change revolving around the problemization of digitization and the loosening up of digital arrangements in higher education.

Jennifer M. Case
Jeroen Huisman

Preface

This book is the result of changing jobs and – for the first time in my career – enduring a lengthy commute to work. All these chapters were sketched out during hour-long train, tram and bus journeys between my home in St Kilda and the main Monash campus in Melbourne's eastern suburbs. This daily trek has given me plenty of time to think about my work – not least the disconnect between my academic interests (broadly speaking, the everyday politics of digital technology) and my twenty years of employment within the university sector. In particular, it soon occurred to me that while I had written, researched and taught a great deal on the use of digital technology within primary and secondary schools, tertiary colleges, households and community settings, I had somehow paid far less attention to what was going on in my own sector of education. As far as I know, there was no deliberate reason for overlooking universities in my previous academic writing. Indeed, as someone who has only ever worked as a university researcher, I have no professional affinity to *any* particular area of education. As such, it is high time that I paid serious attention to digital technology and universities.

As it turns out, my delay in getting around to writing about universities and digital technology has proven rather fortuitous. Higher education is now infused with digital technology to an extent that was hard to imagine even a few years before – from the high-level institutional systems that form a bedrock of university governance and management, through to the almost compulsive use of smartphones and other personal digital devices by academics, students and administrators alike. University campuses are now awash with technological 'kit', and increasing amounts of university work take place in 'virtual' forms. Yet amidst the prominence of these 'digitizations', it is important to recognize digital technology as an extension of the politics of higher education – not least in matters of equality and exclusion; power and the micro politics of the workplace; the correspondences between higher education and global economics; as well as the steady commercialization and privatization of university 'services'. All of these long-standing issues and tensions provide the rationale for this book. Fortunately for me as an author (although less fortunately for me as university employee), this is a book whose time has definitely come.

Of course, unlike many other sectors of education, universities retain deep-rooted and intimate connections with digital technology. Indeed, many forms of digital technology have their origins in university labs. The computer, for example, owes much to Alan Turing's work in Manchester University. Similarly, much software can be traced back to the development of artificial intelligence by the likes of MIT's Marvin Minsky. Indeed, it could be argued that digital technology is one of the most significant 'outcomes' of the heightened post-war investment in European and North American universities during the 1940s, 1950s and the subsequent 'white heat' of technology during the 1960s. Given this heritage, it is ironic to be now considering the consequences (intended and unintended) that these digital technologies are having on the institutional settings from where they were first developed. A number of tricky questions therefore need to be addressed. For instance, what forms of organization and management have grown up within university settings around the use of digital technologies such as the computer and the internet? What are the professional and personal meanings attached to digital technology in higher education? What practices and priorities, understandings and dispositions are associated with higher education in the digital age – both for institutions and the individuals who work within them? These are all questions that this book sets out to tackle.

Before we start in earnest, I feel the need to briefly offer some explanation for two particular forms of terminology used throughout this book. First, like most writing in the area, this book lapses into a conflation of the terms 'university' and 'higher education'. Of course, this is not strictly correct. As Ron Barnett (2011) points out, the notion of a 'higher education' is a critical concept of education that may or may not be found in a university. Conversely, there is a lot more to the institution of the 'university' than higher education. This is clearly a book about universities as institutions. As such the term 'higher education' is used in a broad sense to refer to universities as institutions rather than a specific description of higher forms of teaching and learning. While erroneous, I felt that this conflation was common enough to persist with.

Second – and perhaps less pedantically – it is also worth apologizing for the occasional deployment of the somewhat clumsy phrase 'digital higher education'. This has been used as a means of avoiding having to use even clumsier phrases such as 'the implementation of digital technologies throughout all aspects of universities as institutions'. This book therefore refers to 'digital higher education' in a similar manner to Goodfellow and Lea's (2013) notion of the 'digital university' – encompassing the broad technological and structural changes associated with the increased use of digital systems, devices, applications and tools in higher education settings. In common with the present book, Goodfellow and Lea (2013) see the 'digital university' as a site of considerable tension, 'in which fundamentally different forms of social practice around learning and technologies jostle together and strain the boundaries of institutions and the professional communities that inhabit them' (p.2). Yet, unlike Goodfellow, Lea and the majority of other commentators on technology use in higher education, the present book also attempts to develop a broader perspective on the politics of digital higher education. Here we move the primary focus of attention away from individual experiences of technology-based learning, and focus instead on the wider enmeshing of digital processes and practices with the organization of higher education. Hopefully, these subtle distinctions will soon become clear as the book progresses.

Acknowledgements

Upon moving from the UK to Monash University the contrast of institutional setting prompted me to consider the relationships between higher education and digital technology in a fresh light. While much about the Australian higher education sector is comfortingly familiar to a 'blow in' from Europe, there are also many subtle differences. As such, I have found the change of scene to be continually thought-provoking. In guiding me through these differences, I would like to thank academic colleagues from Monash for humoring my various observations and interpretations. In particular I would like to thank Scott Bulfin for his regular recommendations of further reading. I would also like to thank Michael Henderson, Mike Phillips, Ilana Snyder, Nicola Johnson and other members of Monash's 'Learning with New Media' research group. I have benefitted enormously from working with you all.

Besides these colleagues in Melbourne are a number of other people who previously have played important roles in guiding my reading, thinking and writing. Over the past twenty years I have learnt much from talking about higher education and/or technology with the likes of Keri Facer, Sonia Livingstone, David Buckingham, Martin Oliver, John Fitz and Gareth Rees. While we both worked at the Institute of Education in London, Ambrose Neville was an invaluable source of 'insider' knowledge on the machinations of university information infrastructures. Another person who deserves particular acknowledgment is Charles Crook. As editor of the *Journal of Computer Assisted Learning*, Charles commissioned me to write two articles towards the end of the 2000s that I would have not otherwise bothered with. The first article addressed the problematic nature of digital technology use in universities. The second article considered the need to take a critical approach towards the analysis of education and technology. This book is a belated elision of both these themes – something that Charles clearly saw as worthwhile long before I did.

On a practical note, I am always grateful for the editorial work that goes into the process of book publishing. So, in terms of the production of this book, I would like to thank Jeroen Huisman and Lynn McAlpine for their work in getting this book into the SRHE series on Research into Higher Education. I would also like to thank all of the editorial team at Routledge – notably Bruce Roberts,

Vicky Parting and Sarah Willis for her copy editing. Finally, as is often the case with books like this, all these acknowledgements need to be accompanied by the usual set of disclaimers, caveats and pre-emptive excuses. I would therefore like to remind readers that while this book draws on the work, ideas and arguments of many others, ultimately I am responsible for writing it. All errors, inconsistencies or inaccuracies are mine.

Neil Selwyn
Melbourne, December 2013

Part I

Beyond the rhetoric
of the digital university

Chapter 1

Universities and digital technology

Hype, hope and fear

Introduction

At the heart of this book is a nagging dis-satisfaction with the current state of universities. This, in itself, is not an especially novel or earth-shattering concern. Indeed, this is a concern that has been expressed frequently throughout the past fifty years or so of 'mass' higher education. Thus it is worth reminding ourselves from the outset that 'universities' have been long assumed to be in 'crisis', 'decline' and 'turmoil'. The significant issue that shall be explored in *this* particular analysis is the generally uneasy relationship between the university and digital technology. Of course, digital technologies – most notably computers, the internet and mobile telephony – are now integral features of higher education. These technologies have found their way into most (if not all) aspects of university life, accompanied by far-reaching promises of improvement, innovation and transformation. Yet, looking back to the heady days of the 'micro-electronics revolution' or the 'dot com boom', what shifts have *actually* taken place? What sustained changes have digital technologies brought to universities, and what continuities remain? Have all these changes been for the better? In short, how have digital technologies shaped the character of contemporary higher education, and vice versa? As shall soon become apparent, the answers to these questions are rarely straightforward. This is *not* a book that will be repeating unlikely tales of technological transformation. The realities of higher education in the digital age are far more complicated than many people would like to believe.

Digital technology and the recent 'failures' of higher education

As the twenty-first century progresses, a belief is growing among policymakers, industrialists and educationalists that the traditional model of 'the university' is no longer fit for purpose. This presumption is evident, for example, in the received wisdom that current generations of young people are gaining degrees that leave them ill-prepared for the demands of twenty-first century work and employment. Similarly, the act of studying at university is perceived as a mechanistic and passionless process, with students felt to be 'drifting' through higher education with little discernible effect, and graduating a few years later with no clearer sense of occupational or intellectual narrative. As well as apparently failing in an educational sense, it is also argued that universities are no longer fulfilling their role as centres of innovation and production of 'useful' knowledge. The 'research and development' that takes place within higher education is increasingly dismissed as irrelevant and irresponsive to the needs of the 'real world'. Universities are even felt to have lost their counter-cultural cache as forums for political debate, public conscious forming and general rabble-rousing. In short, universities are no longer believed (if they ever were) to play a useful role in societal, cultural, economic or civic affairs. This leaves the contemporary university in a forlorn state. As John Furlong (2013, n.p.) laments, 'today, universities are very diverse institutions: they no longer have a sense of essential purpose and have largely accepted their loss of autonomy'.

These perceived failings have certainly been exacerbated by the relentless development and use of digital technology throughout society. On one hand, the high-tech industrial sector is now of global economic importance, and technology producers and developers have become prominent 'consumers' of graduate employees. It is ironic that an industry with a celebrated 'college drop-out' heritage (as repeated proudly in the origin stories of firms such as Microsoft, Apple and Facebook) now has a substantial bearing on the fortunes of higher education providers. On the other hand, the relationship between digital technology and higher education is not simply being acted out through the changing dynamics of graduate labour supply. Recent years have also seen a growing belief among policymakers, industrialists and many educators that digital technologies offer a more effective means of 'doing' higher education than the 'traditional' university set-up with its fixed buildings and estates, costly face-to-face procedures and arcane conventions of academic time, space, place and status. This, of course, chimes with a distrust of traditional 'elite' interests and hierarchical, closed institutions that has developed steadily over the past few decades within many sectors of post-industrialized societies. In comparison, growing numbers of people now contend that digital technologies offer a fairer and faster means of higher education provision that is more in tune with the contemporary era (see Castells 2009, Friedman 2007). In this sense, digital technology is increasingly seen as a means of moving on from the inefficient 'producer capture' of contemporary higher education by university institutions rooted in the nineteenth and twentieth centuries.

We have, therefore, reached a point where digital technology and digital culture appear to be bringing the 'problem' of higher education to a head. To draw upon the awkward terminology of high-tech commentators, digital technology might well be the 'game changer' that critics of university systems have been waiting for. On one hand, digital technologies are seen to challenge and question the very essence of what 'the university' is, and what it should be. Growing numbers of critics no longer consider the processes, practices or products of traditional mass-attendance, 'industrial era' universities as fit for purpose. On the other hand, digital technologies are seen by some people as a possible saving grace for universities and those who work within them. Indeed, if some educators and technologists are to be believed, then digital technologies are capable of irrevocably improving and transforming higher education. Although these are complicated (and contestable) issues, one thing seems to be clear – digital technology is an integral element of what higher education now is, for better and for worse. Moreover, digital technology is clearly an integral element of what higher education is to become. For anyone with an interest in higher education, digital technology and digital media are certainly not peripheral or trivial topics to now be considering.

The messy realities of digital technology use within universities

While there is a need to explore the claims and counter-claims that surround higher education and digital technology, it is important to look beyond the hype and speculation that tend to pervade this area. As such, close attention needs to be paid to what has *actually* happened with digital technologies in higher education settings over the past forty years or so. In this respect, while digital technologies are now undoubtedly an embedded feature of universities, we need to also acknowledge that they have *not* yet led to a widespread renewal of higher education. Indeed, despite a superficial high-tech sheen, the institutional essence of most universities could be said to remain remarkably intact from 'pre-digital' times. This serves as a reminder, then, not to assume the relationships between digital technology and higher education to be straightforward or even predictable. The *realities* of higher education in the digital age are more convoluted, complicated and contradictory. To use a term that shall recur throughout this book, the coming together of universities and digital technologies is a decidedly 'messy' business (see Law 2004).

The 'messiness' of higher education in the 'digital age' was brought home to me soon after arriving in Australia at the beginning of 2013. One of the more niche recommended 'must-reads' in the end-of-year newspaper review lists was Richard Hil's (2012) *Whackademia*. Billed as a 'scathing insider exposure' of contemporary higher education, this book had garnered considerable critical and popular acclaim. Drawing on in-depth interviews with mostly anonymous academics, at first glance *Whackademia* appeared to contain little that other university 'insiders' had not long been shouting from the rooftops. Indeed, the book presented a rather drawn out account of working conditions within increasingly bureaucratized universities. Much time was taken detailing the 'drudgery' and excessive 'busyness' associated with a world of 'inputs, targets, key performance indicators, performance management, unit costs, cost effectiveness, benchmarking, quality assurance and so on' (p.10). Seen in this light, the university was portrayed as a 'joyless institution' staffed by 'remunerated zombies' who have been depowered and demoralized through relentless 'over-administration'.

While descriptions such as these might well have come as a surprise to readers and reviewers outside higher education, they are all-too-familiar for anyone working within it. Yet where *Whackademia* did pique my interest was the extent to which this malaise was described as having pervaded everyday life within the university sector – debasing even the most mundane working processes and practices. In this sense, I was especially struck by the manner in which digital technologies featured in the dispirited accounts of Hil's interviewees. Computers, email, the worldwide web, online learning systems and mobile phones, were all described at various points throughout the book as exemplifying the worst aspects of working within modern universities. For instance, the infusion of teaching and learning technologies was portrayed as supporting largely a 'formulaic, Googlized, dumbed-down education' (p.9). As one of Hil's interviewees contended, the mandatory use of virtual learning environments and PowerPoint led almost inevitably to 'mechanical' modes of pedagogy – 'you put up the slides, put your lecture notes online . . . so that your arse is covered' (p.101). Of course, most teachers and tutors remained mindful of the pressures to deploy in-class 'technological pyrotechnics' in order to engage students and thereby boost their all-important end-of-course evaluations. However, this was accompanied by an underlying sense that the self-same technologies were diminishing the quality of teaching and learning.

Digital technologies also appeared to weigh heavily on the research and administrative activities of academics – especially in terms of the 'bleed' of professional life into the domestic sphere. Hil's interviewees bemoaned having to 'frantically labour' at home and in the office – 'seven days a week . . . glued to computer screens' (p.48). Particular scorn was directed towards the digital 'ghost work' of being a dutiful university 'academic' – 'the routine, unacknowledged bits of the daily grind' (p.167) such as answering emails, completing electronic workload formulas, and grappling with online administrative systems. At one point in the book, Hil detailed the electronic 'form proliferation' that had taken hold within one of his previous places of employment – with online permission forms required for actions ranging from booking flights and requesting leave, to being allowed to store alcohol on university premises (p.173). One theme that emerged throughout all these examples was the self-responsibilized and self-accountable nature of these digital work processes – the common bottom line to any demand or query being that the solution could be found 'on the system' (p.106).

Of course, in taking stock of this catalogue of digital woes one has to remember that university academics are notoriously hard-to-please. The default state of most academics is 'disgruntled' – be it in relation to the quality of their staffroom coffee or the state of global politics. Yet even if Hil's book did contain a surfeit of professional whinging, it nevertheless raised some seldom-voiced but legitimate questions about universities and digital technologies. How, for instance, could innovations that supposedly promised a more liberated higher education apparently have had the opposite effect? What had happened to pre-millennial expectations of the cyber-campus and effortlessly 'blended' learning? How had these wonder technologies seemingly got embroiled in the most obstructive and constraining elements of the university machine? Alongside these awkward questions, the one-sided view of digital technology presented in *Whackademia* also raised the need to consider what – if anything – can be done to resist these developments.

After so many pages of digital discontent, any fair-minded reader was left wondering what instances of digital technology use exist within universities that might buck these pernicious trends – i.e. that are genuinely enabling and empowering for those that use them. How could the use of digital technologies in higher education be 'otherwise'?

These questions and issues surrounding the realities of higher education in the 'digital age' are a good starting point for this book. What have been the realities of increasing digital technology use in higher education, and how do these correspond with the long-held promises and potentials of educational technology? What are the realities of digital technology for those who work within universities – i.e. academics, students, administrators and other professional staff? How are digital technologies impacting on the spaces, places and materialities of higher education – i.e. the campuses and classrooms, other learning environments and social spaces? To what extent are digital technologies simply an extension of the organizational, administration and managerial concerns of the university institution? How do these seemingly 'local' issues correspond to wider debates regarding the future of education in the twenty-first century – not least the links between education as a public good, the demands of the global knowledge economy, industry and commerce, and so on? Underlying all these specific concerns is the need to address the broader question that should *always* be asked when critiquing any area of education – i.e. 'what needs to change?'. In other words, how is it possible – if at all – to reconcile the idea of the 'university' for the digital age in a way that retains the core essence of higher education as a public good?

These are all complex issues, and will take some time to dissect and digest. This complexity is an important reason, therefore, for considering the topic of digital technology and higher education in the rather unfashionable form of a 70,000-word book rather than a 500-word blog post or 140-character tweet. While these other media have their uses, this book will embroil itself in arguments that require a relatively generous amount of time and space to be developed. Despite the rhetoric to the contrary, the use of digital technology within universities is not a straightforward issue that will unfold inevitably over the next few years. Instead, there is much to discuss, debate and disagree about. As a contentious starting point, then, perhaps the best way to begin to problematize the current relationship between universities and digital technology is by looking backward. Just what *was* supposed to happen with digital technologies and higher education . . . and how did these expectations eventually turn out?

Making sense of universities and digital technologies – a history of hype, hope and fear

Digital technologies are now an accepted and expected feature of higher education – part of the everyday furniture of universities rather than an exotic novelty. However, it is important to remember that this state of apparent normalization was not always the case. In order to make good sense of the integral position that digital technologies have come to assume within higher education, it is helpful to look back on the claims that were being made – in Carolyn Marvin's (1990) words – in times 'when old technologies were new'. So if we cast our minds back over the past forty years, just what was it that then 'new' technologies were supposed to be bringing to higher education? In short, what could (or should) have happened if everything had gone according to plan, and any of the many technological expectations of the 1970s onwards been realized in full?

Looking back over the past forty years or so, one is struck by the tendency for a majority of commentators to presume that digital technology – most notably computers and the internet – has nothing but benign (and usually inherently beneficial) implications for higher education. Also evident, however, is a recurring minority concern with the degenerative implications of digital technology – especially relating to matters of teaching and learning. Together, these two opposing reactions have long bounded the debates relating to digital technology use in higher education. A useful analysis of these polarized discourses is offered by Chris Bigum and Jane Kenway's critique of the dominant 'boosterist' claims surrounding educational discussions of technology. This boosterism can be characterized as advancing claims of enhanced efficiencies of provision, increased choice and diversity, speed and convenience. As Bigum and Kenway (1998, p.378) described, these were arguments that tended to frame digital technologies as powerful 'drivers' and 'enablers' of educational change and transformation

> characterized by an unswerving faith in the technology's capacity to improve education and most other things in society, often coupled with a sense of inevitability concerning the growth and use of computer technology. They have few doubts about the educational merits of their vision for change.

'Booster' discourses certainly dominated discussions as the first computers began to move out of the computer labs and into offices, classrooms and other parts of the university campus. From Patrick Suppes' (1966) early enthusiasms for the pedagogic benefits of the 'computer tutor' to Tiffin and Rajasingham's (1995) celebration of the 'virtual classroom', predictions of imminent digital transformation of universities thrived within academic, political and popular discussions. Indeed, a succession of educationalists, technologists and other commentators were happy to predict that universities would inevitably follow the lead set by 'dot com'-era businesses and industries into a computer-mediated 'meltdown':

> Developments in multimedia, increased communications and other ICT [information and communications technology] innovations are obviously key components of the information society. In this new era, [university] managers must be prepared to abandon everything they know – and the same may hold for teachers, educationalists, researchers, students and policy-makers. Maintaining the *status quo* is not an option.
>
> (Gell and Cochrane 1996, p.254)

As the urgency of this quotation intimates, the sweeping change of digital technology was felt to apply across *all* aspects of higher education – not least in terms of university management and administration. Yet, if anything, these implications tended to be expressed most passionately in terms of the changing nature of university teaching and learning. As Patricia Breivik (1998, pp.1–3) argued around the same time:

> The seemingly abrupt dawn and speed-of-light growth of the Information Age threatens the very existence of traditional higher education . . . To address th[e] new definition of an educated graduate, higher education must step boldly forward and acknowledge the fact that the traditional literacies accepted in the past as sufficient for supporting a liberal education are now insufficient. In fact, information literacy must be added to the other literacies because students must be information literate to stay up-to-date with any subject in the Information Age!

While often appearing in hindsight as over-wrought and shrill, this 'booster' attitude nevertheless continues to the present day. There is little difference between these past pronouncements and current claims of the imperatives of smartphones, social media, 'the cloud' and 'big data'. Consistent throughout this history of digital hysteria has been a belief that new technologies herald substantial educational change, renewal and – as has become recently popular to suggest – 'disruption' of traditional institutional arrangements (Jarvis 2009, Gallagher and Garrett 2013). One prominent discourse here is the presumed ability of digital technology to stimulate the 'democratic' rearrangement of educational opportunities – in John Daniel's (2009, p.62) words, initiating 'a tectonic shift that will bring the benefits of learning and knowledge to millions'. The notion of digital technology as a democratizing phenomenon is evident in numerous celebrations of the ability of digital tools and applications to allow higher education providers to operate in increasingly 'open' ways, and for individuals to enjoy unprecedented levels of meritocratic educational opportunity. In the words of one UK government minister:

> [Digital technologies] present an opportunity for us to widen access to, and meet the global demand for, higher education . . . new online delivery tools will also create incredible opportunities for UK entrepreneurs to reach world markets by harnessing technology and innovation in the field of education.
>
> (David Willetts, cited in Parr 2012, n.p.)

These booster visions therefore convey a sense of imminent and total transformation of higher education through digital technology. On one hand, then, this involves the digital enhancement of all aspects of university education – from the provision of learner-centred learning, to the pedagogic possibilities of the 'edgeless' institution (Bradwell 2009). On the other hand, from an epistemological perspective, digital technologies have long been associated with the 'freeing-up' of university-produced knowledge. For some educators, then, digital technologies are seen as opening up possibilities for the development of cosmopolitan forms of higher education, 'powerfully contribut[ing] to the worldwide democratization, civic engagement and action-orientated social responsibility' of university educators and their institutions (Benson and Harkavy 2002, p.169). There are many commentators who – motivated by a variety of reasons – continue to argue passionately that digital technology marks a new epoch in the development of higher education – 'usher[ing] in a new era' of what can be seen as 'Education 2.0' (Waks 2012, p.188).

It would be fair to conclude that the dominant discourses around higher education and digital technology are largely positive and uncritical in tone – certainly displaying more optimism than is usually apparent in other areas of educational debate. Yet while such 'boosterism' understandably continues to dominate discussions of higher education and digital technology, this has been countered over the years by a smaller (but no less trenchant) set of what can be termed as 'doomster' discourses. As Bigum and Kenway (1998, p.386) observe, these arguments tend to

> see much damage to society and education arising from the uncritical acceptance of new media forms [. . .] nostalgic for the period when these technologies did not exist or for the practices and institutions that are being replaced by new technologies.

Looking back over the past forty years, these doomster portrayals appear equally as overwrought and alarmist as the optimistic visions just described. For example, an apprehension within some early discussions of the campus-wide introduction of computer technology was that undergraduates might fall too deeply 'in love' with the computer to the detriment of other aspects of their intellectual development (e.g. Evans 1979). Indeed, the 'threat' of computer-based teaching and learning has long provoked suspicion among some pedagogues. As James Kulik and colleagues reflected on the introduction of computers into US colleges throughout the 1960s and 1970s:

> To some critics, computers were expensive gadgets that increased the cost and complexity of instruction without increasing its quality. Others worried that rigidly programmed machines might force all learners into the same mold and stifle idiosyncrasy. Finally, some educators feared that computer requirements would ultimately affect the choice of instructional content. Teachers using computers in instruction, they warned, might be tempted to teach only those things that could be taught easily by machine.
>
> (Kulik et al. 1980, p.525)

Rather than representing a passing phase, such distrust continues to be voiced to the present day, usually in relation to the detrimental influence of digital technology on the quality of university teaching, learning and scholarship. This can be seen in the recurring argument that digital technology use leads to devalued and 'dumbed down' forms of higher education, and an overall 'factory model' of university education with diminished learning opportunities (Cooley 1999). As Rudy Hirschheim (2005, p.101) reasoned: 'if the internet leads to a more standardized, minimalist product targeted for a mass market, this will further "box in" and "dumb down" education, resulting in a system that does not support the endeavors of superior scholars and thinkers'.

Many of the more recent instances of doomster commentary have tended to focus on negative experiences of teaching and learning with digital technologies. Typical of these critiques during the 2000s were Tara Brabazon's *Digital Hemlock* (2002) and *The University of Google* (2007) – books that both attracted a degree of notoriety when published for their headline-friendly criticisms of digital education (such as the contention that internet-based learning was providing university students with 'white bread for the mind'). The latter of these books – *The University of Google* – portrayed a silent majority of undergraduate students who appeared simply to be sleepwalking through their university education and whose potential was stymied by levels of apathy and disengagement that were exacerbated by (over)use of digital technology. Brabazon described these students in an unflattering light as the 'net generation' for whom 'clicking replaces thinking' and scholarship was a matter of 'Googling their way' through degree courses (p.16). In contrast to many booster discourses of the time, Brabazon presented a contrary critique of the worldwide turn towards e-learning, driven by a concern for what she saw as the impoverished learning lives of her digitally distracted students. As Brabazon (2007, p.25) concluded:

> [W]hat I am seeing in my classroom is nearly half of each year's cohort placing education, research and scholarship very low on their list of important tasks. Ironically, in the midst of the knowledge economy, students are being less creative, innovative and dynamic.

As the 2010s progress, similar criticisms continue to be made forcibly and with increased conviction. This discontent often emanates from academics and educators working within universities, as well as from industrialists, politicians, policymakers and the other concerned 'stakeholders'. Take, for example, the lengthy critique of the limitations of digital higher education repeated below. These observations were not expressed in private by a disenchanted tutor on the margins of their institution, but by the newly appointed vice-chancellor of the University of Adelaide at his inaugural public address. When a high-profile university executive (presumably keen to make an initial good impression) feels comfortable to publically direct such criticisms at his own workplace, then the 'doomster' mindset can be said to be as prevalent now as ever before. As the vice-chancellor bemoaned:

They sit in classes often overtired from outside work, distracted by texting friends on ever-present laptops or smart phones, or even gaming which, as one recent study shows, some believe is a legitimate activity in lectures. The digital world impacts students in other ways too. For a decade now fewer have bought prescribed textbooks, believing that if the lecturer's online materials fail to serve, then they can always make do with searching the internet. They are thus ill equipped to read or understand the research literature in their field, and when an enterprising lecturer refers them to a research article, those that read it come away often mystified and irritated at its obscurity, and seldom energized by the idea of the search for new knowledge. The chance that independent research would play a significant role in such undergraduate teaching seems remote. Moreover, the promises of e-learning have not yet captured their attention in ways we might have hoped. They love downloadable lectures, for they like being able to review and revise through that format, being free to skip, highlight, or replay passages as they wish – just as their forebears did with a textbook – or even play at double speed, to make the droning of a particularly ponderous lecturer more interesting. They also like online drills and quizzes where there is instant response. But they complain that other kinds of online learning resources are often poorly executed, boring, or only vaguely related to the subject. Their lecturers are too often not skilled in the full potential of digital resources, using them simply to reinforce or substitute for face-to-face lectures.

(Bebbington 2012, pp.74–75)

Looking beyond the boosters and doomsters

These booster and doomster scenarios have endured over the past forty years, suggesting that when it comes to education and technology many people like to hear little but exceptionally good *or* exceptionally bad news. Yet these depictions do not provide solid foundations for developing a realistic understanding of higher education and digital technology. The consequences of digital technology use throughout higher education have proven nowhere near as clear-cut and certain as either the boosters or doomsters assert. The remainder of this book will do well to set its sights beyond merely updating such 'stories' for the mid-2010s. Yet taking a more sober and circumspect approach does not imply denying the possibility of digitally-related change altogether. Indeed, many sensible and persuasive arguments can be made as to why digital technology might well herald the reconfiguration of 'the university' to some extent. Thus alongside all of the exaggerations and misassumptions just outlined, it is worth remembering that there may well be *some* truth to these booster and doomster scenarios. However, it is also important to remain mindful that the realities of any combination of the technological and the social is always more complex than such rhetoric would suggest.

Notwithstanding this latter point, circumspect accounts of the digitization of higher education are few in comparison to booster and doomster discourses. One such account whose analysis has endured, and therefore offers a useful template for this book's investigation, is a restrained diagnosis entitled 'Electronics and the dim future of the university'. Written by the Columbia Business School professor Eli Noam in 1995 for the high-profile journal *Science*, this reading of higher education and digital technology foregrounded many issues and concerns that have since come to pass in one form or another. In his short piece Noam outlined how information technologies (and, crucially, the economics of information that are associated with them) might influence the main functions of the university – i.e. what he described as 'creating knowledge', 'preserving information' and 'passing information onto others'. Noam was not peddling a determinist notion of digital technology causing these changes per se. Instead he developed a more considered argument that likely substantial changes in the digital production, distribution and consumption of information and knowledge would begin to constitute a viable alternative to the 'slow motion' flow of information through the traditional 'bricks and mortar' university.

As befits a 'dim' reading of the situation, however, few of these changes are described as being straightforward. Indeed, Noam shied away from portraying digital technology in wholly beneficial or wholly detrimental terms, preferring to point out more basic shifts in processes and practices. One of Noam's main arguments was that in an age of 'electronic communities' of 'intellectual collaboration' there would be few reasons for the scholarly creation of knowledge to take place exclusively within the 'physical proximity' of the university. Moreover, it might often be simply more convenient for information to be stored on an 'anywhere, anytime' basis supported via a 'combination of laptop and phone line'. In a similar manner, Noam reasoned that the transmission of this information (i.e. teaching) could well diversify away from the 'low-tech lecture system' to a number of technology-based alternatives. As Noam (1995, n.p.) contended:

> [T]here will be an out-migration from classic campus-based higher education. The tools for alternatives could be video servers with stored lectures by outstanding scholars; electronic access to interactive reading materials and study exercises; electronic interactivity with faculty and teaching assistants; hypertext books and new forms of experiencing knowledge; video and computer-conferencing; and language translation programs.

Twenty years on, Noam's qualified analysis has certainly proved more prescient than the strident booster and doomster scenarios outlined previously, precisely because of its ambiguous and ambivalent approach to the subject matter. According to Noam, the changes associated with digital technology in higher education are neither wholly good nor wholly bad. Moreover, he raises the important contention that many of these technology-related changes would not occur because of any particular effectiveness or elegance, but more 'rationally' because of straightforward economies of scale. As Noam reasoned, 'the point is not that [technology-based forms of provision] are superior to face-to face teaching (though the latter is often romanticized); rather, they can be provided at dramatically lower cost' (n.p.). In this sense, Noam developed a picture of higher education and digital technology that was as much an economic and pragmatic issue as it was a technical or even emotional concern. This led him to foresee, for example, the expansion of provision of higher education to commercial firms and textbook publishers – arguing in essence that the time may well come when McGraw-Hill would be a more successful and recognizable provider of higher education than McGill.

Noam's tempered predictions therefore raise a number of interesting and important points regarding the often uneasy relationship between digital technology and higher education. These include the physical dispersion of people and resources, the corresponding 'outsourcing' of key processes and practices, and the diminishing need for face-to-face interactions. Noam highlights the convenience of some digital practices, and reminds us of the imposed inconvenience of others. His analysis touches upon the tensions between economic efficiencies and academic quality, and also goes some way towards problematizing the increased presence of commercial providers and private interests. It is grounded issues and debates such as *these* (rather than the harried speculations of the boosters and doomsters) that are worthwhile taking forward into the remainder of this book. Twenty years on, what are the intended and un-intended consequences, the simultaneous gains and losses, the continuities and discontinuities of digital technology use in its many forms in higher education? Above all, 'Electronics and the dim future of the university' continues to remind us that such changes cannot be explained away in simple terms of total 'transformation' or absolute 'ruin'. Noam was careful, after all, to predict a 'dim' but not completely 'dark' future. We would be well to be similarly attentive to the complexities of the topic.

Moving beyond the hype – towards a balanced perspective on digital higher education

As this chapter has so far implied, there is a clear benefit in positioning our analysis apart from the narrow concerns, interests and preoccupations of the existing 'educational technology' literature. While useful, much of the body of writing that has accumulated on the subject of higher education and digital technology has either sought to promote and support the potentials and possibilities of 'new' technologies, or else to decry the use of digital technology altogether. Instead, we need to develop alternative readings of the social, cultural, political and economic issues that surround universities and technology. Properly acknowledging the complexity of digital technology and higher education therefore requires adopting an appropriately *critical* perspective, both towards higher education and towards digital technology. This chapter will conclude by outlining briefly the benefits to be gained from the sociology of higher education and, conversely, the sociology of technology. Indeed, these approaches set the scene for the remainder of this book – foregrounding a number of critical issues and concerns that will be expanded upon throughout subsequent chapters.

Developing a good understanding of 'the university'

As should already be clear, much of the presumed significance of digital technology in universities relates to the potential for institutional change and transformation. Key here is a belief that technology offers an unproblematic means of redressing many of the shortcomings and problems that persist within higher education systems around the world. As such, the educational significance of digital technology needs to be contextualized in terms of the reorientation, reconstitution and redefinition of the 'university' over the past forty years. The current significance of digital technology can only be understood, therefore, against the recent backdrop of broader societal shifts surrounding higher education institutions.

Obviously, a number of societal, economic, political and cultural shifts need to be taken into account when making sense of this 'wider picture' of universities and technology-led change. Indeed, changes relating to globalization, the 'knowledge economy' and post-industrialization are all integral elements of this discussion. Thus digital higher education needs to be set against what some commentators would describe as the de-structuring (or at least re-structuring) of society along flexible, fluid, 'liquid' lines (e.g. Giddens 2000, Bauman 2001). As Oxenham (2013) details, key aspects of higher education under these conditions include shifts towards the market-driven consumption of teaching and learning, the shortening life span of useful knowledge, and the changing nature of 'learning' amidst an increasing volume of information. While the exact nature and extent of these changes can be questioned, it is difficult to make sense of any element of higher education without some reference to wider societal shifts in terms of expertise, knowledge, authority, institutions and so on. We clearly need to contextualize our discussions of higher education and digital technology accordingly.

There is much to be gained, therefore, from approaching digital technology in terms of the sociology of higher education (see David and Naidoo 2013). This highlights 'perennial questions about higher education, including its social organization, purposes, structures, practices, and divergent impacts on participants in the enterprise and on society at large' (Gumport 2007a, p.325). One of the strengths of the sociology of higher education is its nuanced portrayal of the many recent demographic, economic, ideological, organizational, political and professional changes to the institutional realities of universities (Gumport 2007b). Significant here, for example, are perennial concerns of social class, gender, disability, inequality and identity. As such, the sociology of higher education draws attention to the diversity of provision and practice within the umbrella term of 'higher education', and warns against over-generalized or homogenous accounts of 'the university', 'students' and so on.

In particular, the sociology of higher education highlights the importance of exploring – rather than ignoring – the complexities and tensions arising from the continuing massification of university education around the world. At a basic level, for example, it important to distinguish the many different forms of 'university' that exist – from Ivy League institutions to community colleges, from research-intensive to mass teaching organizations, from private liberal-arts colleges to specialized institutes of technology. There are, for example, around 4,500 higher education institutions now operating within the US. Similarly, there has been a threefold increase in universities in the UK since the 1960s – currently numbering 109 'university' institutions accompanied by another 133 other higher education institutions. These trends are being replicated around the world, with the global number of university students forecast to rise from 99.4 million in 2000 to 414.2 million in 2030 (Calderon 2012). Among these all rapid expansions it is important to remain aware of the great diversity of 'university' institutions that now constitute the higher education 'sector'.

As well as drawing attention to quantitative changes such as these, the sociology of higher education also highlights a range of more subtle social reconfigurations of university working environments. For example, recent sociological studies have detailed the changing nature of the 'student experience' of studying within massified university systems – highlighting, for example, the pressures of balancing part-time employment with part-time study, or the experiences of new generations of 'non-traditional' working class students (see Case 2013, Lehmann 2013). Similarly, studies have also highlighted the reconfiguration of professional roles – not least the changing nature of faculty work towards fixed-term, part-time, non-tenured positions. Indeed, in the UK, more than one-third of academics are now employed on temporary contracts as universities look to casualize their workforces. In Brazil, the proportion of faculty who are on short-term, part-time contracts is closer to 80 per cent (Fazackerley 2013).

The sociology of higher education therefore draws attention towards what Gumport (2007c) describes as the 'changing contours' of universities and university life. Here, there are at least two levels of shaping influence that are of relevance to our later discussions. First, at a 'societal' level of analysis the sociology of higher education highlights the importance of the 'business' of higher education, reminding us that contemporary universities are centres of teaching, learning and scholarly research that also operate as multi-billion dollar quasi-corporations. It also reminds us that universities are situated within complex political contexts – with the liberal dispositions and sensibilities associated traditionally with university culture (as apparent, for example, in periodic expressions of campus protest, faculty strikes, the spirit of 1968 and so on) contrasting with dominant neo-liberal concerns of commercialization and corporatization.

Second, these changing contours of contemporary higher education are evident at an 'organizational' level of analysis. These include the increasingly complex nature of university governance and management – as embodied in the extensive administrative systems now to be found in any university. This is also reflected in the diversity of functions that universities have – with many institutions moving away from their traditional 'core' functions of teaching and 'pure' research, and towards 'knowledge transfer', business development and other forms of entre-preneurial activity and pursuit of 'innovative' ventures. Concurrently, universities have seen the reorganization of their teaching and learning activities, with a grow-ing emphasis on the instrumental value of studying knowledge. This has involved the reorganization of undergraduate and graduate curricula along 'applied' lines to meet student and employer demands for vocational preparation. These shifts clearly contrast with traditional 'scholarly' concerns of teaching and learning for its own sake, e.g. to develop character, cultivate citizenship, promote cultural literacy and so on.

There is much, therefore, that this book can take from the recent concerns of the sociology of higher education – not least what has been described as 'critical university studies' (Cantwell 2013). This is an increasingly prevalent perspective that challenges the erosion of the public purpose of higher education – problema-tizing the increased privatization of previously 'low-cost' or 'no-cost' forms of university education as well as the increased role of marketization and market val-ues. This approach therefore seeks to re-conceptualize what public higher educa-tion could (and should) be – suggesting a focus on the re-establishment of higher education as 'a public service, a social entitlement, a space for critical thinking and a place of discovery' (Bailey and Freedman 2012, p.10). As Brian Cantwell (2013, p.x) concludes:

> There is value to research and scholarship that might be considered 'critical university studies' [. . .] Major tasks include identifying problematic elements of academic work, teaching and learning, and university management and governance, but also theorizing and identifying the ways in which alterna-tives might be realized.

Developing a good understanding of digital technology

Alongside a sociologically sophisticated understanding of higher education, it is also necessary to pursue a critical understanding of digital technology. Most academic writers are now well aware of the limitations of taking an overtly deter-ministic perspective on education and technology. Yet an underlying sense of tech-nological determinism persists with such tenacity within popular, professional and academic discussions of educational technology that it bears repeating that these descriptions inadequately reflect the complex shaping relationships between the social and the technological. Put bluntly, to assume that digital technology some-how has an innate ability to 'change' higher education is a nonsense. Instead, any observer is better advised to approach higher education and digital technology as *mutually shaping* – i.e. influencing each other in ways that are driven by a range of influences and interests (see Wajcman 2002). As Bill Dutton (2013, p.179) details, we therefore need to concentrate on 'the ways in which people – users, developers, policy-makers, managers, and more – shape technology, which itself is a social as well as a technical system'. Moreover, due acknowledgement needs to be given to the role of 'various institutional contexts, which motivate, structure, and otherwise constrain' technology uses (Dutton 2013, p.189). As such, we should recognize from the outset that digital technology is clearly not an uncontested or uncontroversial area of education, but rather an intense site of conflict.

Thus higher education and digital technology is best perceived as a set of struggles that take place across a number of fronts – from the allocation of resources and design of curricula, to concerns with the maximization of profit or equality of educational opportunities. As Wiebe Bijker (2010) reminds us, 'how to use technology?' is an inherently political question. Seen in this light, many of the key issues underpinning higher education and digital technology would appear to be political questions that are asked continually of education and society – i.e. questions of what is education, and questions of what education should be. Developing a fuller sense of how and why digital technologies are being used in university settings therefore demands recognition of broader issues of conflict, control and resistance. In short, any account of digital technology use in higher education needs to be framed in explicit terms of societal conflict over the distribution of power.

Approaching educational technology in this manner therefore demands a willingness to engage with the negative – as Apple et al. (2010, p.5) put it, 'to illuminate the ways in which educational institutions, policies and practices are connected to the relations of exploitation and domination – and to struggles against such relations – in the larger society'. In this sense, any study of digital technology and higher education would undoubtedly benefit from adopting a pessimistic rather than optimistic mindset. This is not what Michael Burawoy (2011) identifies as an 'uncompromising pessimism' that is engaged with for its own sake. Instead what is being suggested here is that digital technology use within higher education is approached from a position that expects nothing. The pessimistic commentator is therefore willing to accept that digital technology is *not* bringing about the changes and transformations that many people contend. Similarly, the pessimistic commentator recognizes that to imagine otherwise for the future is to misunderstand the nature of social change. Yet this is not to approach the use of digital technology in higher education as an inevitably hopeless endeavour. Instead, pessimism offers a realistic basis from which the recasting of digital technology use in higher education can take place. As hopefully will be evident by the end of the book, by taking pessimism rather than optimism as the starting-point for our analysis, we should eventually be in a good position to explore how best to work alongside and within the imperfections of digital technology and higher education.

Thus it makes sense for the remaining chapters to approach digital technology use in higher education from a position akin to Gramsci's notion of being 'a pessimist because of intelligence, but an optimist because of will' (Gramsci 1971/1929). In other words, unlike the ultimately dismissive 'doomster' positions outlined earlier, this should be a pessimism that recognizes the benefits of starting from a position that acknowledges the parameters and boundaries of any technological endeavour, and holds realistic expectations of the struggles and conflicts that surround any social change. This knowledge might *then* be used to go on to inform political action conducted in a more optimistic spirit. Yet as John Holloway (2002, p.8) reasons, 'if the hope is not grounded firmly in that same bitterness of history, it becomes just a one-dimensional and silly expression of optimism'. Pessimism can provide a powerful basis for exploring ways that digital technologies can be used by individuals to better survive within inherently imperfect situations. It is therefore a fitting way of approaching the vexed topic of 'digital higher education'.

Conclusions

This chapter has set the scene for the remainder of this book, identifying a number of issues that will be expanded upon subsequently. First and foremost, it has been argued that one cannot make good sense of contemporary higher education without paying serious and sustained attention to 'the digital'. However, this is accompanied by a need to look beyond the exaggerated rhetoric that continues to dictate how digital technology and higher education are imagined in popular and political circles. Instead, there is a pressing need to concentrate on the less spectacular and seemingly more mundane, everyday realities of digital technology use in higher education. As such, it is important not to be distracted by what are relatively peripheral trends and niche activities. Despite talk of the 'virtual' university and 'massive open online courses', enrolments in classroom-bound courses delivered on 'bricks-and-mortar' campuses by mass-enrollment university institutions continue to grow across developed and developing countries alike. Similarly, while an elite cadre of globally mobile students undoubtedly *are* studying around the world in 'nimble' and 'nomadic' ways, many more less-privileged students are having to attend local institutions, regardless of the better options that might be found further afield. Real-life, face-to-face, embodied research processes and practices continue to over-shadow the unconstrained promises of 'e-research'. Amidst these various slowing-downs and speeding-ups, digital technology is neither heralding a whole-scale renaissance of higher education practices and processes nor causing the end of the university as we know it.

So it seems sensible that this book proceeds in an appropriately circumspect manner. As has just been argued, this involves being purposively pessimistic rather than unrealistically optimistic. It should be clear by now that developing a good understanding of the relationships between higher education and digital technology requires looking beyond the rhetoric of possible 'effects' and anticipated outcomes. Instead, we need to think carefully about what is *actually* taking place in the traditional university settings where the vast majority of 'higher education' activity still takes place. This involves thinking about how digital technologies are implicated in – and entwined around – the everyday processes and practices of higher education institutions. Once viewed along these prosaic lines, then it quickly becomes apparent that the realities of higher education in the digital age are far less extraordinary than are often described. This is not to say that the consequences and connotations of digital technology in higher education are any less important, significant or worthy of our attention. It is just that the digital 'transformation' of higher education is nowhere near as straightforward or clear-cut as we often are led to believe.

Chapter 2

Digital technology and higher education 'reform'

Introduction

As implied throughout Chapter 1, it makes little sense to approach digital technology and universities in context-free terms. Any aspect of higher education is enmeshed with shifts in global economics and national politics, as well as various societal and cultural (re)formations. This chapter therefore examines the interplay between digital technology and the social, political, economic and cultural contexts of 'higher education'. Continuing the distinction between 'societal' and 'organizational' influences, the chapter will examine three distinct elements of the societal level of analysis. First is the increased globalization of economic, financial and cultural processes. Second, is the corresponding rise of the so-called 'knowledge economy'. Third – and perhaps most significantly – is the rise to prominence of neoliberal ideology and the increased bearing of new forms of managerialism on the nature of higher education over the past forty years.

All of these wider societal rearrangements are key to understanding how digital technologies have found a place within contemporary universities. Indeed, it can be argued that the ever-increasing presence of digital technology within higher education is both driven *by* these wider contextual changes, and a driver *of* these wider contextual changes. Yet it is important to acknowledge from the outset that the 'imaginary' of the hyper-globalized, knowledge-producing, market-driven, technology-rich university does not wholly accord with the digital practices that take place 'on the ground'. As was stated regularly throughout Chapter 1, the realities of digital technology use within higher education are often constrained, compromised and contradictory. This chapter will therefore highlight a set of contextual issues, which can then be taken forward into subsequent chapters. Once we have a clear understanding of the contexts of contemporary higher education, then fully making sense of the complexities of digital technology use will become that much easier.

The changing nature of 'the university' – globalization, the knowledge economy and the rise of neoliberalism

Universities have faced unprecedented political, economic and societal changes over the past forty years – a point that is overlooked in most discussions of higher education and digital technology. In particular, universities have borne the brunt of continuing globalized shifts in economics, finance and governance. Put simply, these wider contextual changes leave the 'university' of the 2010s bearing little resemblance to the 'university' of the 1970s or 1980s. These are institutions that now 'compete' within 'marketplaces' for students, research funding and other forms of income. These are institutions that are concerned with efficiency, enterprise and innovation. These are certainly not bastions of Humboldtian liberal education and academic freedoms. The 'university' of the early twenty-first century is a very different prospect than it would have been even twenty years previously.

From one perspective, the nature and form of contemporary higher education has been shaped by ongoing worldwide changes with regards to production, consumption and investment – what is commonly referred to as globalization. Universities are now positioned within global 'flows' of ideas, information, practices, institutions, objects and people. This is especially relevant with regards to the increasing interconnectedness of economic markets and steady establishment of 'global common markets' over the past forty years. In industrial terms, for example, the production of goods and services now takes place through international markets and worldwide circuits of trade and exchange. In financial terms, the past forty years have also seen the expansion of new worldwide financial markets. Global demands for sufficient quantities of skilled labour are also of continued importance – not least the consistent demand for high-skilled 'intellectual' workers. All of these issues have obvious implications for the business of universities in terms of the 'production' of graduates and the 'production' of knowledge.

As such, contemporary higher education is embedded within a range of globalized processes – not least a confluence of interactions, ideas, institutions, knowledge and skills. As Melanie Wilson (2010, p.182) contends:

> There is little doubt that the impact of globalization on higher education has reshaped and continues to reshape the landscape of academia. Universities are increasingly more connected as global research initiatives become more commonplace; global university rankings influence university mandates and focus; global trade impacts publicly funded universities; and faculty and students can teach and learn in new globally networked ways. This changing landscape has challenged universities and colleges to revisit their *raison d'être*, all while remaining viable in this new global context.

Wilson touches upon a number of important features of globalized higher education. For example, she conveys a sense of higher education as a fluid, continuous and competitive process for institutions and individuals alike. She also highlights the shaping of the financial fortunes of universities by global trade in research and knowledge production. Conversely, the focus of educational provision is described in terms that reflect the growing significance of the intellectually-based head work of the knowledge economy as opposed to the manual body work of the industrial economy (Brown et al. 2011).

As Wilson's description also suggests, many of these changes relate to changing expectations of how higher education is to be delivered. The received wisdom of 'lifelong learning' dictates that educational provision is no longer expected to be bound solely by the dominant institutional forms of the school, college and university, or to the dominant life-cycle of childhood to late adolescence and early adulthood. In a practical sense, it is now presumed that education is a lifelong concern that takes place inside and outside of formal education systems. Conversely, from an epistemological perspective much of Wilson's description also reflects the ongoing 'crisis of meaning' for university institutions in a world where traditional markers and boundaries of 'culture', 'knowledge' and 'understanding' no longer hold the significance that they once did (Readings 1996).

Recent globalizations of finance, economics, information and ideas, culture and peoples therefore present fundamental challenges to established notions of the form and function of higher education. It is here, then, that the notion of the global 'knowledge economy' is another important aspect of making sense of the contemporary university. In simple terms, the knowledge economy refers to the increasing significance of the production and manipulation of information and knowledge rather than the production of physical goods and services. As Chakravartty and Sarikakis (2006, p.22) argue, the knowledge economy 'symbolizes a transition from the manual/machine-assisted production line of material things to an abstract, placeless interaction between human and electronic brains for the production of services'. Following this logic, the production and distribution of knowledge and information is now a core component of economic growth and, therefore, changes in employment. As a consequence, the capacity of organizations and individuals to engage successfully in learning, training and 'reskilling' processes becomes an increasingly important determinant of economic performance (Pantzar 2001).

The knowledge economy thesis therefore implies that individuals and organizations face major educational challenges in ensuring their economic success. Thus it is recognized by policymakers and employers alike that access to higher educational opportunities has implications not only for general economic competitiveness of countries and companies, but also for the employability (and associated standard of living) of individuals. A dominant view has emerged in many countries and regions that the effective organization of educational opportunities is a crucial driver of economic growth. The emphasis on individuals within the knowledge economy model reflects a 'human capital' understanding of individuals participating in learning according to their calculation of the net economic benefits to be derived from education and training (Becker 1975). As Brown et al.

(2008, p.132) reason, the essence of this human capital approach is that 'income reflects the level of skill'. Given the prevailing view of contemporary economic change as predicated upon knowledge-based forms of production, human capital theory therefore sees individuals seeking to participate in higher education in order to capitalize upon the labour-market benefits that should result from skills renewal and development. In this sense, the main challenge that individuals are required to address throughout their lives (or at least throughout their working lives) is the ability to accrue the skills required for success in the labour market. Perhaps as importantly, this also involves the ability to accrue the associated certification and accreditation. When seen along these lines, the main challenge that universities are required to address is the provision of educational opportunities that allow individuals to participate in the required education and training and accumulate the resulting skills and qualifications.

As these latter descriptions suggest, universities now find themselves as integral but subordinate components of a fast-changing global economic landscape. Whether described in terms of globalization or the knowledge economy, it is difficult to overlook the links between higher education, national economies and global economics. The beliefs and values underlying most forms of recent change and reform within higher education have therefore been simple ones. In terms of how university teaching and learning is arranged, these issues can be summarized as: (1) that a knowledge economy requires an information-skilled workforce in order to succeed; and (2) that the key to an information-skilled workforce is increased participation in higher education and learning. In addition, from the perspective of economic productivity, individual universities and national systems of higher education have key roles to play as profitable sources of knowledge production. In both these senses, as Roger Dale (2005, p.118) has noted, the knowledge economy is therefore 'intrinsically related to education'. As such, it is not hard to see where digital technologies fit with these wider imperatives and agendas.

Yet in describing the changing contexts of contemporary higher education we should take care not to be completely economically driven. These 'economic' shifts have been accompanied by less direct (but no less substantial) adjustments in the ideological bases of higher education – in particular the rise of 'neoliberalism' as a dominant system of ideas and values. As an ideological form, neoliberalism extends libertarian notions of individual liberty, self-responsibility and personal entrepreneurism with an explicit belief in consumer choice and market freedom, coupled with the dominance of private interests over the workings of the state. For many commentators, neoliberalism is now a well-established and dominant ideology across all industrialized societies. As David Harvey (2005, p.3) contends, neoliberalism 'has pervasive effects on ways of thought to the point where it has become incorporated into the commonsense way many of us interpret, live in and understand the world'. Indeed, despite the global economic crises of the late 2000s and early 2010s, neoliberal ideology has proved remarkably adaptable and resilient. As Michael Peters (2011, p.5) continues, neoliberalism 'is undeniably still the ruling ideology even though it has transmuted in form a number of times'.

In making sense of the bearing of neoliberalism on recent forms of higher education, it is important to distinguish between the often flawed application of neoliberal ideology in practice and its more abstract form as what Charles Taylor (2004) describes as a 'social imaginary' – i.e. as a set of ideas and ideals. In this latter idealized form, neoliberalism can be understood as a powerful but largely unrealized project seeking to remould the world in its image. In this abstract sense, neoliberalism 'involves a broader range of underlying principles, ultimately political values that are deeply embedded' (Couldry 2010, p.22). Key here is the primacy of unrestricted individual action, individual responsibilization and values of self-interest, individual entrepreneurialism and competition (Hilgers 2010). From this perspective, the best means of preserving individual freedoms while also establishing societal order is understood to be the 'spontaneous order' of the market. This leads to an emphasis on 'choice' and relations of 'competition' as the most efficient means of allocating resources, as well as the most efficient means of achieving human freedom (Munck 2005). As such, neoliberalism seeks to privilege individual self-concerns over any responsibility of institutions and the state. The role of institutions is reduced, at most, to supporting strong private property rights, free markets, free trade and the entrepreneurial activities of individuals (Harvey 2005). Again, it is not difficult to see how these individualized, 'free' and 'open' interests and agendas map onto enthusiasms for various forms of digital technology use that are similarly individually driven.

New universities for new times?

These issues have all had profound bearings on the nature and form of the contemporary university. Contemporary higher education is now seen to be aligned closely with issues of global economics and economies, commercialization and privatization, commodification and markets. On one hand, these changes are evident in the operation of universities along more 'business-like' lines. Indeed, it could be argued from an organizational perspective that there is little to distinguish the management and governance of higher education institutions from private firms or small corporations. This is certainly apparent in the governance and management of higher education. Universities are now presided over by a new elite class of managerial professionals in the form of highly-paid and hugely-powerful executive directors, vice-presidents and deputy vice-chancellors. These positions are accompanied by multiple layers of middle-management in the form of directors, coordinators, registrars and team leaders. This 'corporatization' of higher education is also apparent in the vast expansion of any university's functions – from the massification of student numbers, increased pursuit of research funding and other expansions into new markets and territories.

Indeed, the modern university can now be characterized by its positioning within wider higher education 'marketplaces' and its general ambition to make universities more 'market-like' and run along market-led lines. As Simon Marginson reminds us, these are 'quasi markets' rather than '*bona fide* capitalist markets' – with universities supposedly benefiting from the presence of internal markets, without being subjected to the full force of commercial competition. Nevertheless, as Marginson (2013, p.353) continues: 'For more than two decades, governments around the world, led by the English-speaking polities, have moved higher education systems closer to the forms of textbook economic markets. Reforms include corporatization, competitive funding, student charges, output formats and performance reporting.'

Thus while not fully-fledged market organizations, universities are now increasingly conceived and operated along competitive lines. As Cantwell (2013, p.152) observes, 'universities that were once sites of learning and discovery are now engines of economic competitiveness and places where students invest in their human capital'. Indeed, it could be argued that universities have become subsumed by the 'language of economics' – i.e. 'the language of accountancy, finance and economics: the language of "the market"' (Smith 2012, p.650). Conceived along these lines, universities are concerned with the efficient logistics of educational provision, coupled with the maximization of market-share and profitability. Accordingly, students are positioned in the role of consumers, while universities are positioned in the role of providers. As such, the university is defined as an enterprise, 'producing a set of commodities, [albeit] services rather than physical products' (Aspromourgos 2012, p.44).

Some commentators have described this commodified recasting of modern higher education as heralding the emergence of fully-fledged 'entrepreneurial universities', engaged in the pursuit of 'academic capitalism' (Slaughter and Leslie 1997). This sees universities not simply responding to pressures to be more 'business- *like*' in their operations, but to actually 'become a business' (Barnett 2011, p.39). The notion of the entrepreneurial university was popularized by Burton Clark, with the term being used to illustrate the ways in which higher education institutions have been 'pushed and pulled by enlarging, interacting streams of demand, [and] pressured to change their curricula, alter their faculties, and modernize their increasingly expensive physical plant and equipment – and to do so more rapidly than ever' (Clark 1998, p.xiii).

The idea of the 'entrepreneurial' university certainly captures succinctly the diversifying ways in which universities are now organized – pursuing the establishment of links with business and industry sectors, developing favourable positions in markets for student recruitment and research funding, and generally striving to operate as globally referent organizations. The 'entrepreneurial university' also implies a sense of venture and risk-taking in the pursuit of increased capital – reflecting the engagement of many universities in commercial activities such as contract research and consultancy, commercial development and 'knowledge transfer'. It has been argued by many critics that these facets of academic 'enterprise' tend to be centred on the 'aggressive pursuit' of economic opportunities (Rhoades 2007, p.115), and are thereby shaped increasingly by values associated with a residual pressure to 'search out new sources of money' (Deem 2003, p.293). As this chapter begun by noting, universities are clearly very different places to live and work within than they were even twenty years ago.

The realities of contemporary higher education – the rise and rise of New Public Management

As will be apparent to anyone who recently has spent time within a university setting, higher education is shaped profoundly by these 'new' economic pressures and neoliberal sensibilities. Yet to reiterate what was argued earlier, it is important to recognize the clean abstracted ideals of the knowledge economy and neoliberal 'imaginary' as separate from the often-flawed application of this ideology in practice. As many commentators have pointed out, practical application of neoliberal ideology within educational institutions is often at odds with idealized notions of individual freedoms, 'open' action and the efficiency of markets. Thus, in order to understand fully the context of contemporary higher education, we need to consider what Stephen Ball (2012, p.2) describes as the 'how' of neoliberalism – i.e. 'how it is promoted, how it is done'. In practice, what Ball (2012) terms 'ordinary, everyday' neoliberalism is associated with a set of 'mundane practices' based around a market-mentality and values of individualized responsibility, enterprise and entrepreneurism, market solutions and consumer choice. This is what Aihwa Ong (2007, p.4) refers to as neoliberalism with a small 'n' – i.e. the everyday processes and practices within an organization that are based around 'reconfiguring relationships between governing and the governed, power and knowledge'. Crucially, this has tended to be realized most commonly in educational contexts through what critical commentators have portrayed as a pernicious commodification of practice:

> [A]t its most visceral and intimate, neo-liberalism involves the transformation of social relations into calculabilities and exchanges, that is into the market firms, and thus the commodification of educational practice – e.g. in economies of student worth, through performance-related pay, performance management and flexibilisation and labour replacement. Neo-liberal technologies work on us to produce 'docile and productive' teachers and student bodies, and responsible and enterprising teacher and student selves.
>
> (Ball 2012, p.29)

In higher education, these neoliberal techniques of commodification and control have been manifest in the guise of what has come to be termed 'New Public Management' (NPM). As Rosemary Deem (2001) details, the growth of new managerialism within the public sector stemmed from the restructuring of welfare services in countries such as the United Kingdom and New Zealand during the 1980s. In practice it involved the application of management techniques, values and practices derived from the private sector of the economy to the management of publicly funded organizations. On one hand, then, new managerialism is concerned with the simple translation of market values and dispositions into public organizations. Thus these practices could be seen as aligning neatly with the abstract neo-liberal 'imaginary' – conveying the benefits of free markets, private business enterprise and the freedom of the individual consumer. On the other hand, however, new managerialism has tended to involve the 'rigorous' imposition of market forces, business discipline and managerial control techniques within all of the major facets of higher education organizations. These include techniques such as the establishment of internal quasi-markets, processes of quality management, auditing and accounting, contracting out of services and functions, and so on – all constituting regimes of management and governance that 'oscillate between centralized strategic direction and devolved local control' (Deem et al. 2007, p.9). As Simon Marginson (2013, p.354) observes, the practical application of NPM contains an awkward combination of free-market values and bureaucratic control:

> NPM is a hybrid set of organizational practices. It is not a simple function of neo-liberalism and has multiple roots. It combines neo-liberal business models and market templates, with on one hand bureaucratic control systems that emphasize audit and accountability, and on the other hand ideas of transparency and individuation that owe as much to the 1960s New Left as the 1970s New Right.

Recently some commentators have suggested that NPM techniques are being superseded in many areas of the public sector and civic society by collective, self-organized ideals of 'neo-technocratic managerialism' or 'digital era governance' (Dunleavy et al. 2006). Yet this certainly does not appear to be the case in most higher education settings. Indeed, the management and governance of universities continues to be centred on the widespread use of managerialist 'control technologies' – i.e. sets of 'plans, recipes, through the rules and instruments for the governing of behaviour inculcation of certain "understandings" of how the world is and how it should be worked on' (Deem et al. 2007, p.12). These include various forms of control over university administration, culture and work, manifest in audit, performance and accountability technologies such as workload management systems and student satisfaction measures. Recently, for example, UK universities have been required to collect and publish a set of fifteen 'key information sets' for each of their taught programmes that can then be used by potential students to judge the character and quality of different courses (Barnard et al. 2013). Developments of this kind suggest that NPM remains a more defining presence within higher education than has ever been the case previously.

Thus as far as many educational commentators are concerned, the dominant model of the contemporary university is less that of the entrepreneurial university than the 'bureaucratic university' – i.e. institutions that are characterized by 'steering' mechanisms, systems of 'command and control', 'evaluative governance', supervision, regulation and a distinct 'shift [in] power to consumers and managers' (Ferlie et al. 2009, p.13). As Ferlie and colleagues conclude:

> [T]he NPM relies on markets . . . rather than planning; strong performance management, monitoring and management systems, with a growth of audit systems rather than tacit or self-regulation, and empowered and entrepreneurial management rather than collegial public sector professionals and administrators.
>
> (Ferlie et al. 2009, p.13)

As this book progresses, therefore, we need to contrast the idealized imagined lines of expansive and efficient forms of 'digital higher education' against the rather more constrained institutional realities of the university contexts in which digital technologies are actually being used. This certainly involves looking beyond the outward-facing, reputation-enhancing 'corporate' poses that many universities affect when it comes to presenting publically their 'innovative' digital practices and high-tech institutional identities. Indeed, from the day-to-day perspective of working within higher education, the university (and by extension the digital processes and practices of the university) is most likely to be experienced in terms of its rules, regulations, requirements and rigid management and governance structures. As Ron Barnett (2011, p.46) concludes, 'this is university life lived out by the proforma – it is the rule of the proforma'. While care must be taken not descend into a 'doomster'-like disavowal of *all* things digital, it is nevertheless important that any analysis of digital technology is located firmly within the full, flawed context of higher education.

The idealized place of digital technology in the neoliberal university

All these recent shifts in the nature and character of universities have been realized in many different forms – from the language that is now used to describe and discuss higher education, to the physical appearance and arrangement of university campuses. However, all of the contextual changes and shifts outlined in this chapter can also be seen to involve digital technology in one way or another. As shall be demonstrated throughout this book, digital technology is now a core element of the management, organization and governance of any university, regardless of its institutional size or status. The centrality of digital technology is manifest, for example, in the use of complex digital portals and databases to support teaching, learning and research processes. It is also apparent in the use of digital technologies to support the coordination of management and administrative procedures. Conversely, digital technology is embodied in terms of the information technology (IT) professionals now employed to manage digital technology within the contemporary university. In many universities, technology is managed centrally under a 'chief information officer' (or suchlike) who will oversee numerous organizational units connected to various missions such as 'teaching and learning', 'corporate services', 'security' and so on. Individual academic faculties and departments will also have their own IT staff employed in similar roles. Digital technologies are now a central element of what universities do, and how (and through whom) they do it.

As far as many external observers and 'stakeholders' are concerned, these 'digitizations' of higher education are leading inevitably to the complete transformation of universities as they currently exist. Take, for instance, a recent research report from the influential consulting firm Ernst and Young (2012). Unequivocally titled *University of the future: a thousand year old industry on the cusp of profound change*, the starting point of this synopsis was the bleak observation that 'the current university model – a broad-based teaching and research institution, with a large base of assets and back office – will prove unviable in all but a few cases'. The report went on to identify five 'drivers of change of this brave new world'. These included what was characterized as the 'democratization of knowledge and access' (apparently as a consequence of 'massive expansion' of online resources); the 'contestability of markets and funding' (apparently due to declining public investment in higher education provision); 'integration with industry' (apparently through work-integrated learning and the funding of applied research), and 'global mobility' of students and staff. Underpinning all these changes, however, was a fifth 'driver' – i.e. the presence of digital technologies. As the report reasoned:

> Digital technologies have transformed media, retail, entertainment and many other industries – higher education is next. Campuses will remain, but digital technologies will transform the way education is delivered and accessed, and the way 'value' is created by higher education providers, public and private alike.
>
> (Ernst and Young 2012, p.4)

The Ernst and Young report went on to identify a number of distinctly corporatized ways in which digital technology is set to support the 'streamlining' of how universities operate. This was described in business-like terms of universities' assets and holdings, their 'product', 'channels to market' and 'delivery mechanisms'. The report therefore detailed the integral role of digital technology in supporting the reconstruction of the university along all these profoundly neoliberal lines. It talked of the diversification of markets for university teaching and learning through online courses – i.e. what the report described as 'bringing the university to the device'. Conversely, it talked of using personalized digital technologies throughout campus-based learning – i.e. 'bringing the device to the university'. It described 'streamlined' university institutions 'invest[ing] heavily in digital sales and delivery channels' (p.16) – both 'pure play' digital channels and 'blended' models of provision. Notwithstanding its predilection for business jargon, the Ernst and Young report offered a stark glimpse of the ways in which many influential people and interests see digital technology leading the university sector.

These views are increasingly common amongst policymakers and educational commentators. A recent UK think-tank report authored by Michael Barber and colleagues outlined a similar set of incoming challenges (or as these authors put it bluntly, an 'avalanche') faced by contemporary universities. These included a warning that 'the global economy is changing' – particularly in terms of international forms of production and the increased emphasis on 'immaterial' goods and services. Similarly, readers were reminded that 'the global economy is suffering' – with increasing levels of unemployment amongst young people and increased disparities in wealth. Alongside these broader economic shifts, the report then went on to highlight a number of failings inherent in current higher education arrangements – i.e. the facts that 'the cost of higher education is increasing faster than inflation'; 'the value of a degree is falling'; 'content is ubiquitous' and 'competition is heating up' from non-university providers of what were once traditionally university-provided products and services (Barber et al. 2013). Faced with these imperatives, universities were argued to have little option but to reinvent themselves as organizations or face an increasingly uncertain future. Unsurprisingly, digital technology was heralded as a key factor in this reinvention:

> University leaders need to take control of their own destiny and seize the opportunities open to them through technology . . . to provide broader, deeper and more exciting education. Leaders will need to have a keen eye toward creating value for their students.
>
> (Barber et al. 2013, p.5)

The messy realities of universities and digital technology

The breathless certainty of such diagnoses, and the presumed centrality of digital technology to the transformation of higher education along neoliberal lines is all well and good. Yet the fact remains that pronouncements such as these (however persuasive and plausible they might appear) simply are not being borne out in the vast majority of higher education settings. 'Edgeless' institutions and 'pure play channels' may well exist in some specific circumstances and forms, yet these are largely imagined, idealized and highly aspirational elements of the current higher education landscape. In reality, the majority of instances of 'digital higher education' as they have been *actually* realized and implemented are far more mundane and messy. Indeed, the realities of digital technology use in higher education usually bear witness to the clumsy intertwining of (potentially flexible) digital forms with the rather more fixed realities of the university campus, bricks and mortar lecture theatres and seminar rooms, and the rigid constraints of time-tabling systems and semesterization. The imagined freedoms of digital higher education are more often than not compromised by long-standing organizational, bureaucratic and disciplinary realities that are distinctly non-digital in their origins.

The key point to make here, therefore, is that the digitally-supported transformation of the university is by no means smooth or predictable. It is simply not good enough to proclaim blithely that universities are 'on the cusp of profound change' or facing a technological 'avalanche'. Any changes associated with the use of digital technology in higher education are likely to be incremental, iterative and often unforeseen. Indeed, perhaps the most certain predication that *can* be made of any implementation of digital technology in higher education is that it is likely to involve a number of 'non-effects' as well as far-reaching unintended consequences. For example, as Ron Barnett (2011, p.35) observes of the ostensibly 'entrepreneurial' trend for universities to invest in the transfer of their teaching to online modes of delivery:

> A university may decide, for example, to establish computer-based variants of all of its programmes of study, or even determine substantially to switch its 'portfolio' of courses in that direction. This will incur high up-front costs, not least in the training and development of its faculty, quite apart from the installation of the more physical infrastructure. The venture, undertaken seriously, has profound implications for the university: its pedagogies change, its educational relationships with its students change, the relationships that the students have with each other change (the students may become more interactive among themselves) and the pedagogical identity of the 'tutors' change (less a visible authority, aided by an immediate physical presence, and more an enable of learning tasks and opportunities). It follows that, in addition to the surface changes that entrepreneurialism heralds, changes also occur at a deep level. Indeed, in our present example, the university changes as such. It is not merely that the students are less visible on campus; now, this university is marked by new kinds of identity (of both students and tutors), relationships and communicative structures.

As this example suggests, the 'business' of higher education is simply too complex to be improved unproblematically by the application of digital technology. To reiterate the stance taken towards the end of Chapter 1, it is unrealistic to imagine the inadequacies of higher education as party to neat and discrete technical fixes. Of course, Barnett is by no means the first commentator to make such observations of the 'messiness' of the realities of digital higher education. As we shall see through the remaining chapters of this book, there is an established body of critical writing advancing these arguments, yet to seemingly little avail in terms of how higher education and digital technology continues to be talked about in most popular, political and professional circles. Indeed, to reiterate another point made in Chapter 1, it would appear that few people like to be reminded of the obvious complexities of the realities of digital technology use in education.

Conclusions

The complicated and compromised picture of higher education and digital technology that has been developed throughout this chapter highlights a set of enduring issues that will now be taken forward into the rest of this book. With the ever-increasing amounts of money, resourcing and effort now being directed towards the technological transformation of universities around the world, it is time to consider the forms that 'digital higher education' is actually taking on the ground, and therefore problematize what otherwise is being presented to us as 'fact'. The critical commentaries highlighted in this chapter remind us of the need to identify problematic elements of the ongoing digitization of contemporary higher education – whether in terms of working conditions, the provision of services (such as teaching or research), or institutional management and governance. Recalling one of the central justifications for the pessimistic perspective that was introduced in Chapter 1, there is also a need to theorize and identify the ways in which alternatives might be realized. A key point to bear in mind throughout the remainder of this book, therefore, is that 'despite the exigencies of markets, entrepreneurialism, bureaucracy and globalization and shifting knowledge structures and identity structures that characterize universities, they still have options before them' (Barnett 2011, p.4).

And so we can move forward onto the substantive heart of the book. Continuing the distinction between societal and organizational influences, the next four chapters will examine various 'organizational' aspects of digital higher education – i.e. the virtual systems and material spaces that constitute 'the university', as well the experiences of those people (academics, professional staff and students) who work within the university. Analysing *all* these factors – from the 'macro' to the 'micro' aspects of digital higher education – should then place us in a good position from which to make sense of the messy realities of higher education in the digital age in the concluding two chapters. First, then, we need to consider the many 'digital systems' that now underpin what is the contemporary university, and how it operates. What does it mean to have increasing amounts of university information and interaction mediated in online, virtual forms?

Part II

The realities of universities and digital technology

Chapter 3

Digital systems

Digital technology and the organization of universities

Introduction

One of the key points that shall be developed throughout the next four chapters is that much of what 'digital higher education' involves is not particularly digital in either its origins or outcomes. The three chapters *after* this one will focus on the people and the places, the objects and the experiences of working with digital technologies within universities. All these chapters will demonstrate the insights that arise from focusing less on the digital technology per se, and more on the 'real-life' aspects and implications. That said, this current chapter is a little more technology-centred – concentrating on the digital 'systems' that are now used to mediate many of the processes and practices of higher education. Indeed, the increased digitization of universities over the past few decades has seen most aspects of the 'business' of higher education mediated through digital systems. These are perhaps most prominent in terms of the digital systems used to coordinate and manage teaching and learning within universities. However, digital systems are now used for most aspects of the organization, administration and management of universities. This chapter considers all these 'virtualities' of universities in the digital age – unpacking the nature and outcomes of the 'virtual turn' within higher education. As will soon be apparent, this is not a particularly technology-dominated discussion. Ultimately, as we shall see, these digital systems are just as connected with 'real-life' issues as everything else that shall be examined throughout this book.

These digital systems will be familiar to anyone who has spent even a brief period of time working or studying in a university. Like many 'embedded' technologies, often these systems are only apparent when they are encountered as an outsider. Indeed, one of the immediate sticking points of working in any university setting where you are not an employee is being included (even temporarily) in the systems to allow you to log-on to the computer networks, gain access to certain rooms and buildings or make a claim for travel expenses. Similarly, one of the frustrations of starting a new university job or enrolling to study on a course, is the so-called 'on boarding' process of new personnel and students being entered onto institutional systems. This involves an endless pantomime of creating user

IDs, personal numbers, passwords and security checks in order for the incoming individual to be eventually recognized on the key institutional systems. These systems include online payroll and finance accounts to ensure that an individual is neither in the university's credit or debt. These systems also include campus smart card systems for accessing buildings, using libraries, photocopies, printers and anything else is capable of having a card reader attached to it. Perhaps most problematically, these systems will also include any number of IT and computer user accounts. While all these systems are essentially the same from university to university, they can initially seem foreign and unfathomable to anyone being newly enrolled. Then, after a few weeks or months, these systems recede into the background of everyday university life. Yet, as such initial awkward experiences should remind us, these systems are a fundamental aspect of the digitization of contemporary higher education, and are imbued with issues of power, control, regulation and organization. They are, therefore, an ideal place to commence our analysis of the imperfections of universities in the digital age.

Digital systems of university teaching and learning

The digital systems just described are encountered regularly by teachers and students. It is now rare that a university course will not be 'supported' or 'facilitated' by one (or more) digital system. Most commonly this takes the form of the 'learning management systems' (LMSs) and 'virtual learning environments' (VLEs) that are now used as platforms for information and resource sharing, as well as the organization of curriculum and pedagogy. These systems follow on from more ad hoc arrangements during the 1990s and 2000s where course information and resources were shared through bespoke course websites and departmental 'intranets'. In contrast, the current generation of LMS and VLE technologies are seamless, sophisticated applications that seek to replicate the main functions of the university in digital form. These systems support the provision of learning content and other resources, communication between learners, teachers and administrators, the submission and assessment of coursework, and the monitoring of learning progress. The most popular of these applications – in particular the commercially produced 'Blackboard' system and its open source competitor 'Moodle' – are now used widely throughout universities and colleges as a preferred means of managing and administrating nearly all aspects of the teaching and learning process.

Of late, these virtual technologies (which are concerned specifically with the organization of curriculum and pedagogy) have been blended with digital systems designed to support the routine processes of data collection, record-keeping, monitoring and assessment, creation and distribution of learning resources, and coordination of students, teachers and administrators. These technologies include 'management information systems' that collate record-keeping functions such as payrolls, budgeting and accounting, lesson timetabling, scheduling and planning, as well as the management of student admissions, registration and attendance.

The past ten years or so have seen the increased convergence of these 'institutional' technologies into integrated systems – thereby allowing data, resources and other services to be accessed and used across the different aspects of a university organization. This has seen the integration of management information systems, VLEs and communications technologies into virtual systems that are accessible to educational managers, administrators, teachers *and* students. As such, college and university use of integrated management and administration-related systems now represents a significant feature of universities around the world.

While traditionally these teaching and learning systems have been 'closed' to be accessible only by those students from within the university who had paid to enroll on a particular course, there has been a recent trend within many universities to also use digital systems for the provision of 'open' courses and the unrestricted delivery of educational programmes. There has been growing interest in traditional university institutions offering free online courses and instruction supported by various forms of online learning management systems. Early examples of this included the 'AllLearn' consortium of Oxford, Yale and Stanford universities offering over 100 online enrichment courses, proceeded by the later Stanford University 'Introduction to Artificial Intelligence' open course and the $60million 'edX' programme run by Harvard and MIT offering certified university-level courses. Now through commercial companies such as Coursera and Udacity, individual university courses are offered to worldwide audiences of students – all delivered and managed through the companies' online learning systems, often referred to as 'massive open online courses' (MOOCs), and being facilitated by academics and faculty around the world. These systems use a combination of online content management systems, group forums and other content sharing software to facilitate online courses for large numbers of dispersed students – often involving video lectures from invited faculty and experts accompanied by readings and discussions.

While diverse in nature and form, all these virtual systems are perceived to have a number of common benefits and advantages. For many commentators, these virtual systems introduce increased freedoms to any individual's engagement with education. A prominent argument in this respect is the benefits of personalization and flexibility for individual learners. For example, the virtual provision of teaching and learning is often argued to provide individualized forms of instruction that better serve the specific needs and learning styles of students. Virtual learning systems are seen to allow flexibility in terms of scheduling and place, as well as expanding high-quality learning in specific subjects. While some students actively will choose to enroll in virtual programmes and courses, the online provision of education is also seen to play a compensatory role for students who are unable physically to attend 'bricks and mortar' institutions. As such virtual provision of university teaching and learning is justified as a ready alternative for students who are in full-time employment, or with extensive family and caring commitments, are either geographically remote or mobile, or who are otherwise unable (or unwilling) to meet the regular time and place demands of 'traditional' university study. Even when students continue to attend physical educational provision, virtual learning systems are seen to extend the provision of the formal educational institution into all other contexts of students' lives (e.g. work, home, travelling) and allow for additional learning opportunities when outside of the classroom.

Virtual teaching and learning systems are also celebrated as providing students and teachers an enhanced freedom from the physical constraints of the 'real-world'. This is often expressed in terms of the overcoming of barriers of space, place, time and geography with individuals able to access high-quality educational provision regardless of their local proximity. Additionally, virtual systems are described as offering individuals an increased social and psychological freedom from their real-life circumstances. Enthusiasts argue that virtual systems and online learning therefore have profound implications for the ways that students and teachers can communicate and interact with each other, with people no longer constricted by distance, time or physical attributes such as location or body. In this sense, it is argued that users can construct diverse 'virtual identities' and forms of virtual embodiment through which they can experience these 'virtual' worlds. The key advantage here being that the individual user has control over both their environment and their presentation of self.

Besides these individual benefits, the virtual provision of university education is also seen to increase a number of institutional efficiencies. This is particularly the case with the outward facing 'open' provision of courses to worldwide audiences through MOOCs. Here digital technology is seen to be increasing choice and imposing 'market accountability' in the form of competition that drives educational providers (both online and offline) to improve as they compete to recruit and retain students (Miron and Urschel 2012). As such, the virtual provision of courses is often justified as increasing the (beneficial) presence of market efficiency and competition into universities – both in terms of internal competition between different programmes within a university, and in terms of external competition between different institutions. Indeed, virtual courses and programmes have tended to be developed and run by a variety of providers – from consortia of universities, to small private companies and large multinational corporations. Growing numbers of commercial companies also act as vendors for the delivery of virtual courses and the licensed use of virtual course materials. This 'learning marketplace' is bolstered by the considerable amount of content developed by educators and universities themselves and provided through platforms such as iTunes U, YouTube.Edu and Academic Earth. All told, the virtual provision of teaching is seen to make university education more diverse and more competitive. This reflects what the technologist Chris Anderson (2009) identified as the 'long tail' of digital provision, where purely digital products that are of marginal, niche interest can be produced and consumed at no additional material loss.

These issues all feed into the wider contention that virtual systems can support what Bill Gates once termed 'friction-free' interactions and experiences between producers and consumers of university education. While Gates was talking primarily about the reduced environmental impact of virtual rather than material forms of production and consumption, this notion of friction-free benefit is often applied in social terms – reflecting 'an impression of digital space as a radically democratic zone of infinite connectivity' (Murphy 2012, p.122). These claims are accompanied by a sense that virtual technologies support forms of education that are somehow more efficient than would otherwise be the case. Purported benefits of VLEs, for example, include the increased 'engagement' of students with 'personalized' educational provision, the 'democratizing' of educative processes through the flattening of traditionally hierarchical relationships, and increased levels of institutional 'performance' and teacher productivity through the 'open' sharing of learning administration and management data (see Selwood and Visscher 2007). All in all, the increased mediation of teaching and learning through these virtual systems is now established as an accepted – and expected – feature of contemporary higher education.

Digital systems of university administration and organization

While these teaching and learning systems are perhaps the most familiar and high-profile aspects of digital technology for university teachers and their students, they are just one aspect of the extensive digitization of organizational processes within the contemporary university. As was pointed out regularly during Chapters 1 and 2, modern universities are extensive organizations – turning-over millions or billions of dollars each year, managing extensive estates located around the world, employing tens of thousands of staff and engaging with hundreds of thousands of 'customers'. As such, the governance and management arrangements required to sustain these levels of activity are considerable. Like many other large-scale and complex organizations, universities have long made use of computer-based 'institutional technologies' to support the routine processes of data collection, record-keeping, monitoring and assessment, coordination of human resources. A variety of digital systems therefore lie at the heart of all university administrative processes – from academic and student support and administration to business development, the organization of finance and human resources, information services and technology provision, marketing, research administration, quality assurance and other forms of 'compliance' faced by large publically-facing organizations. As this exhaustive list suggests, all aspects of the 'business' of the modern university will now have a digital dimension.

While differing in appearance between universities, these systems tend to conform to similar standards and specifications – often being commercially produced systems that have been adapted for public-sector organizations, or developed specifically for educational institutions. Computers have, of course, long been used for record-keeping functions such as payrolls, budgeting and accounting, room-bookings, timetabling, scheduling and planning, as well as the management of student registration and admissions. Now, however, these systems are increasingly integrated into overarching systems for broad areas of university administration.

One such example is that of 'Student and Administrative Management Systems' (SAMS) – systems designed to cover every aspect of the university's official contact with a student. These systems will therefore be used to handle initial admissions enquiries and applications from prospective students, enrolment, records of achievement, accounting and budgeting, and eventually graduation and alumni records. A student's entire contact with the university organization will be covered through one 'profile' on such a system.

Similar systems will handle a university's personnel and employment records, with so-called 'e-HRM' technologies integrating human resource management functions from 'talent acquisition services' to 'performance management' and 'compensation management' (Bondarouk and Ruël 2009). These systems are often used to support 'workload management systems', which are used to quantify and apportion responsibilities and duties throughout the academic and administrative workforce. These systems are deployed (often contentiously) to establish 'models to allocate and monitor' the work of academics and professional staff (Kenny et al. 2012). This strategic use of digital systems feeds into the wider use of a variety of 'management information systems' to highlight and support managerial planning and decision-making. University leadership and management is now reliant upon 'Decision Support Systems', 'Executive Information Systems' and 'Enterprise Resource Planning Systems' – all designed to consolidate and synthesize data from a wide range of sources, which is then used to support decision-making and future planning.

Indeed, university governance and management is now reliant increasingly on digitally based methodologies, processes and architectures designed to transform disparate data relating to the university organization into meaningful and useful information – often in the form of 'ideal' models of business and organizational 'best practice'. These systems are used for processes such as 'business intelligence', 'learning analytics', 'data mining', 'predictive analytics' and 'complex event processing' (see Ferguson 2012). For example, universities are beginning to collate and combine data that arise 'naturally' from students' interactions with course websites, library services and face-to-face meetings with teaching staff. These 'learning analytics' and 'academic analytics' are being used to inform curriculum design, class planning and the kinds of learning support offered to different groups of students (Swain 2013).

While the internal, 'back-room' running of these aspects of organizational management and administration has long been technology-based, the use of digital systems to take care of their 'front-facing' aspects has also grown. Thus it is now commonplace for any 'end-user' of these systems to have to interact with them through another virtual system – usually an online 'portal' or university intranet. In this respect, much of the discontent reflected in Richard Hil's insider accounts of university working conditions in Chapter 1 was not far off the mark. Most universities now use online compliance systems for every aspect of university work – including routine requests for leave, booking travel tickets, and specific compliance issues such as the bringing of alcohol onto university premises. This process often commences on the first day of anyone's employment in a university through the digitally-based induction of new staff members. Here, new employees are taken through the various stages of employment compliance, financial require-ments, required training (covering everything from health and safety through to dignity and respect in the workplace) and registration of details for everything from pension schemes through to library membership.

These digitally-mediated processes continue through one's career at a univer-sity. They also increasingly characterize any dealings with the external institutions of higher education – i.e. research funding councils, professional accreditation bodies and learned societies. For example, the extent of proliferation of these external and internal digital systems in the working lives of university academics and administrators is illustrated by the life-cycle of any research project – one of the core 'products' of the university. The succession of steps in the research proj-ect process can take place almost exclusively through digital means – from the ini-tial proposing of a project and bidding for funding, to the final dissemination of results and reporting of findings. Most funding councils, for example, have com-pletely automated digital systems for the preparation and submission of funding proposals, ensuring compliance with requirements ranging from the calculation of the budget through to the number of words and font size of the proposal docu-ment. These systems are used to coordinate the peer reviewing of the proposals, and eventual administration of successful grants. Researchers and research admin-istrators will then deal regularly with these systems over the lifetime of a project to cover ethical clearance for data collection, submission of regular progress reports and evidence of achieving 'milestones', and eventual submission of datasets and final reports. One can complete a major multi-million dollar research grant with-out once interacting directly with a person working for the research funder. The entire process is digitally supported and virtually enacted.

There are seen to be many benefits of this widespread virtualization of uni-versity organization and governance – often along the lines of establishing uni-versities as 'smart' organizations on a par with other similarly sized businesses in the commercial and industrial sectors. At one level, these 'efficiencies' involve the direct replacement of human labour with digital equivalents, the reduced use of material resources (what Bondarouk and Ruël (2009) term 'filing cabinet replication'), and the redistribution of tasks to individual non-specialists. A key 'efficiency', in this latter respect, has been the shift in secretarial and clerical work to individual academics. This internal redistribution of work is also accompanied in some instances by the external 'outsourcing' of functions to 'lower-cost and higher quality providers' (Hillman and Corkery 2010, p.13) – especially in areas such as marketing and recruitment, as well as in areas such as instructional design and course development. Moreover, as implied in the descriptions earlier, these systems are also seen as a key means of supporting analytical modeling, plan-ning and decision-making. In this respect, digital systems are implicated with wider turns towards managerial practices of 'change management' and 'service improvement'. As Behenna and Schulz (2011, p.19) put it, these digital systems are now seen as an essential means 'to respond to external and internal drivers around quality, excellence, compliance and effectiveness, significant investment of resources to improve the way academic work is supported, and part of the drive to improve business practices and service levels continuously'.

Problematizing the prominence of digital systems in higher education

Of course, despite such idealized descriptions and imagined benefits, all of these systems need to be made sense of in profoundly problematic terms. As anyone working in a university will know, the systems outlined above rarely operate smoothly. These systems are replicating highly complex data structures and work processes, meaning that they inevitably are frustrating to deal with as well as technically difficult to maintain. More fundamentally, however, are a set of deeper-rooted concerns over the social, political and cultural roles of these systems in mediating the university organization. Thus, despite the rhetoric of these systems serving to 'empower' individual learners or 'support' individual employees, it must be remembered that these are primarily 'institutional technologies' – i.e. technological systems that are used to support the 'formalized, technically developed, and rationalized procedures that regulate the everyday operations of institutions' (Griffith and André-Bechley 2008, p.43). Seen in this light – and with the pessimistic stance raised in Chapters 1 and 2 fresh in our minds – there are a number of critical issues and concerns implicit in the role and function of these digital systems within universities. In brief, these centre on the following three issues.

Systems of replication and rationalization

One the central claims of many of these digital systems is that they somehow support 'new' forms of organization – usually along more efficient, effective and even 'disruptive' lines. Yet rather than instigating significant changes to management and governance processes, or the provision of teaching and learning, it would seem that these systems more often than not serve to reproduce long-standing and deep-rooted structures and arrangements of 'the university'. It could be argued, therefore, that all the various forms of digital systems just described tend to replicate (rather than disrupt and alter) offline processes and practices. These continuities are perhaps most obvious with the digital systems of teaching and learning. For example, most forms of VLE, MOOC and the like mark the institutional persistence of their offline equivalents in terms of organization and administration, social relations and culture. Within a VLE, for example, learners are often positioned in ways similar to any face-to-face form of formal education – i.e. as passive consumers of resources and instruction, as individuals who are formally assessed, whose attendance is required and whose collaboration with other learners is expected to follow the largely artificial conventions of 'group work' and seminar-style discussions that remain 'on topic'. It is telling that within even the supposedly least constrained virtual educational settings, learners will still often be found to be re-enacting the rituals of offline learning processes – printing off papers and books, setting self-imposed schedules and maintaining strict division between curriculum domains of knowledge. As McKnight (2012, p.373) observed of the governance structures that tend to be chosen by the online 'communities' that arise within virtual worlds, 'managerialism is the norm'. In this sense, virtual teaching and learning systems are not so much of an escape from the constraints of traditional education structures, routines and conventions as an entrenchment of them.

That the established traditions and tropes of 'traditional' education remain largely intact in these virtual systems certainly goes against the prevailing rhetoric of freedom and diversity – especially in terms of university teaching and learning. Indeed, there is very little evidence of a prominent 'long tail' of esoteric, niche and obscure learning opportunities being made available to potential consumers in virtual form. Rather, it could be observed that virtual systems support 'more of the same' educational provision. As such, VLEs, LMSs, MOOCs and the like appear to be doing little to challenge or disrupt what David Tyack and William Tobin (1995, p.454) refer to as the basic 'grammar' of formal education – i.e. the combination of material artifacts and social relations 'designed to instruct, socialize and discipline' learners and therefore providing the dominant underpinning 'structural framework of pedagogical practice' (Brehony 2002, p.178). This grammar of formal education includes the persistent structures and rules that divide time and space, classify students and allocate them to groups, and splinter knowledge into 'subjects'. Indeed it is notable how many of the virtual educational systems highlighted in this chapter echo the almost subconscious way that rules and approved 'ways-of-being' are internalized, adhered to and often reproduced by those who work within 'traditional' higher education institutions – not least the principles of standardization, order and hierarchization.

These observations chime with general criticisms that most forms of 'virtuality' that are supported by digital technology tend towards replication, standardization and homogenization. As Murphy (2012, p.133) reasons, most virtual technologies tend to be immaterial expressions of material practices and processes – 'an intensification of the old' rather than the purveyors of anything 'new'. Critics such as Campanelli (2010) therefore see digital systems as little more than replicating of reality in a more visible data-driven form – at best leading to 'the progressive aestheicization of reality' rather than offering any genuinely alternate arrangements. Thus despite the rhetoric of change and opportunity, digital systems – whether for university teaching or university administration – could be seen as representing 'a parallel reality that overlaps and replaces physical reality . . . Life happens in an unrelenting visibility and – mostly thanks to digital media – in a perfect (numeric) transcription' (Campanelli 2010, p.60).

Thus in contrast to the transformatory claims outlined at the beginning of this chapter, the realities of online, computerized systems need to be understood in terms of continuities with the traditional, offline, concrete forms of teaching, administration, governance and management that both preceded and continue alongside them. Woolgar's (2002) mantra of 'the more virtual the more real' is certainly relevant here – reminding us that engagement in digital processes usually stimulates more engagement with the 'real-life' processes that they replicate. For example, the 'convenience' of virtual teleworking usually is associated in practice with more real-life physical travelling. It may therefore make more sense to see digitalization and virtuality – as Jordan (1999) suggested – as the reinvention of familiar physical realities and spaces in digital online settings, rather than any radical break with what went before.

Of course it would be wrong to claim these digital systems support *exactly* the same practices, processes and procedures as their offline concrete forms. Instead, all of the digital processes and practices outlined in this chapter can be seen as reduced, simplified versions of what are complex administrative and educational processes and practices. However, this distillation is not necessarily for the better. For example, the clean lines of the online course omit a wealth of detail that otherwise gives character, vitality and meaning to a real-life 'messy' classroom. VLEs often offer abstracted icon-based representations of the core activities of learning and teaching, omitting all manner of informal and tacit processes and practices. The same can be said for the systems used to calculate and model workflows and workloads, which attempt to quantify activities and actions that are socially, emotionally and personally complex in ways that cannot be described fully by numbers. Any computer-based staff orientation and induction system, however sophisticated, can appear dead-eyed and lacking in emotional depth when set against the realities of the setting it seeks to simulate. In short, it could be argued that digital systems tend to offer abstracted, decontextualized and ultimately diminished replications of higher education processes and practices.

At their heart, then, any form of digital system at use within a university setting needs to be understood as a simulation of a physical, concrete form of higher education practice, with all of the reductions and restrictions that simulation entails. Indeed, Edward Castronova (2006) proposed the description of 'synthetic' rather than 'virtual' as a means of acknowledging the essentially replicated and reduced form of any digital system. Although these technologies do combine impressive amounts of audio, gestural and haptic information, they are largely visual in nature – offering what Castells (1996) terms 'symbolic environments' that are based predominantly around the image. In this sense, digital systems could be seen as presenting necessarily abbreviated and simplified versions of the complex processes and practices that they seek to represent and simulate. Brian Massumi (2002), for example, dismisses the forms of virtuality supported by digital technologies as artificial 'sweeping gestures' that bypass the sensations, movement and affect of the processes that they seek to replicate while systematizing the possible number of pre-defined outcomes. Other critics have described these technologies as presenting a 'simulacrum' of an object (Murphy 2012), undermined by their tendency to reduce complexity to the level of 'something already known' (Krapp 2011, p.2).

In this sense, the computerized systems that now constitute the digital university could be said to involve a number of limitations, restrictions and omissions. First, these systems often appear to present unrealistically straightforward and unproblematic versions of the real-life processes and practices that they seek to replicate. As Bauman (2010, p.15) observes, 'the main attractions of the virtual world derives from the absence of the contradictions and cross-purposes that haunt offline life'. Digital systems could also be said to present users with limited forms of choice and action. As Campanelli (2010, p.92) notes, despite the 'founding myth' of interactivity, digital systems are only capable at best of offering the user an 'infinite number of finite options'. All these technologies – from the most sophisticated 'decision support system' to the most expansive VLE – are predicated upon designer created hierarchies of 'choice'. The restricted 'scripted' nature of any computerized system is therefore influenced by how the application developers and designers have configured the technology for the imagined 'ideal' users. As Campanelli (2010, p.94) continues, this can leave a virtual system as a frustratingly 'castrated form' for all but the most unremarkable of users:

> [D]esigners impose a one-size-fits-all model upon what is, in fact, a chaotic mass of non-aggregated users. The search for formal standardization and the effort towards the homogenization of interfaces have produced 'castrating forms', which bridle the individual's creativity as they interact with different interfaces.

Seen in this light, it could be argued that digital systems tend to support enclosed rather than open forms of action, thereby positioning individuals into 'pre-defined relationships and structures, which are reproduced and reinforced through even the most trivial statements and actions' (Friesen 2008, p.10). This is often evident the way in which VLEs tend to position individuals in a role of 'the student' (producing work, being assessed and monitored) or 'the tutor' (providing resources, grading assignments, monitoring participation). These roles, and the 'scripts' that are associated with them, tend to be laden with unequal distributions of power and control. As Friesen (2008, p.10) continues, once 'positioned' in these roles, 'individual identity is to some extent defined by them'.

All these issues therefore highlight the generally abstracted and decontextualized nature of engaging with universities as institutions through digital technologies. In this sense, parallels can be drawn between virtual spaces and Marc Augé's (1995) notion of the 'non-place'—i.e. places of transience that do not hold enough significance to be regarded as real-life, sustained, meaningful 'places'. In his original work Augé was focusing on locations such as the airport terminal, supermarket, hotel room or motorway as some of the primary non-places of modern times, yet the argument could be made for the virtual university spaces described above as having similar transient, decontextualized characteristics. Here, then, all individuals (be they managers, administrators, students or professors) are assumed to be 'average', divested of their real identities and backgrounds, on the assumption that their needs can be catered for through a process of mass customization. Whereas these digital environments and spaces may claim connections with concrete equivalents in the offline world, they are not integrated with the history of these predecessor places but simply seek to appropriate their memory. As such, many of the digitized forms of teaching, administration and governance reviewed in this chapter could be seen as little more than 'the university' with the (old) life and colour sucked out of it. It is of little surprise, therefore, that these are abstracted forms that more often than not descend into 'banal utopias, clichés' (Augé 1995, p.95).

Systems of control

The second issue that runs throughout our descriptions of these digital systems is their role as systems of organizational control. The function of these systems to replicate and rationalize the processes and practices of higher education clearly reduces the range of possible actions to any individual who is interacting with the system. Thus, rather than being open-ended and intuitive, these are more accurately seen as systems of social rationality – bound by a series of rules and offering a limited number of options to the individual – and therefore producing an inherent 'institutional order' similar to other systems of social rationality. As has already been suggested on a few occasions so far in this chapter, the realities of these systems are often structured and constrained in nature. These are systems that usually do not encourage interactions that are especially 'interactive' in the usual sense of the word – i.e. where 'the viewer has the power to be an active participant in the unfolding of a work's flow of event, influencing or modifying its form' (Lovejoy 2004, p.167). At best, the interactivity of these virtual systems is best described as involving top-down impositions and 'false modes of active engagement' (Fuery 2009, p.33).

Thus, despite their associations with individual empowerment and interactivity, these digital systems tend to be used along rational and repetitive lines, with users adhering to strict rules and developing bounded strategies in order to proceed. Of course, most would consider the sophisticated and expansive systems being used currently within universities to offer substantially more variety and freedom of action than their predecessors of even ten years before. Yet the fact remains that even the most sophisticated and carefully designed digital systems retain an inherent rationalization of action. By its very nature, therefore, using any digital system is entwined with issues of power and control – not least the capacity of the individual user to make empowered choices and act in meaningful ways. Apperley (2009) suggests that the complex dynamic between the user and any digital system is 'fraught with subtle negotiations of power', which reflect wider and long-standing tensions between institutional control and individual agency. In the case of many of the systems described in this chapter, these tensions relate clearly to the long-standing division of universities along lines of 'education' and 'resource' decisions. As Simon Marginson (2000, p.34) reminds us:

Clearly the old idea of collegial governance, whereby academic staff govern the university, administer it and provide some of its auxiliary services, is obsolete. . . . Competitive pressures, efficiency imperatives, and requirements as to transparency and accountability ensure that administration, management and professional service functions must be carried out by professionals. These professional general staff are as important as are academic staff to the long-term health of their institutions. . . . Resource decisions (the domain of managers) and educational decisions (the domain of academics) are always closely implicated in each other. Without a stable collaborative relationship there will be tendencies for one group to try to secure control over the other's functions.

What *does* appear to be new about the digital systems described in this chapter, however, is how these tensions are now codified in the programming of these applications. It is noticeable how these digital systems tend to be configured in ways that are often signified heavily in terms of traditional university roles, regimes and relationships, and imprinted with power-related agendas and 'scripts' that define appropriate behaviours and interactions. As such, these digital systems can be seen as spaces where university governance, management and administration is performed and 'acted out'. Beyond these performative roles, these systems render social power and control through a succession of highly symbolic data-driven processes. The computerized systems described in this chapter are an integral means through which universities are now executing their main data-based 'batch processing' functions – i.e. the monitoring and control of bodies (be they employees, visitors or 'customers'), assignment of tasks to staff and students, and subsequent enforcement that these tasks were completed.

These systems can therefore all be seen as an important element of the 'data turn' in higher education that is a key element of the NPM. In particular, these systems should be seen as a tangible embodiment of the recasting of universities over the past two decades along more business-orientated centralized 'data-driven' lines. We now have higher education systems that are based around the creation and use of data that support the organization of political relations through communication and information. In terms of use of data within an individual university institution, there are well-established systems of self-evaluation, development planning and performance. These include data-driven processes of internal management; performance management of academics and administrators alike; target setting; addressing underperformance; and student monitoring and tracking. In terms of use of data across educational systems there are similar processes and practices – from national student satisfaction surveys, national performance 'league tables', national quality audits such the UK 'Research Excellence Framework', international 'indictors' such as the QS World University Rankings, and any number of other systems of data comparison and diagnosis. As Jenny Ozga (2009, p.154) has noted, 'this process is relentless and inescapable'.

The intentions of this data turn are deliberate – not least the intentional move towards what Ozga terms 'governing education through data' and the shift from central regulation to individual self-evaluation:

> Data production and management were and are essential to the new govern-ance turn; constant comparison is its symbolic feature, as well as a distinctive mode of operation . . . The shift to governance is, in fact, heavily dependent on knowledge and information, which play a pivotal role both in the per-vasiveness of governance and in allowing the development of its dispersed, distributed and disaggregated form.
>
> (Ozga 2009, p.150)

In this sense, data are now an integral component of the new governance of uni-versities and those who work within them along neoliberal principles of decentral-ized and devolved forms of control. As such, the most significant measures of any individual or institutional 'success' are now expressed in terms of the data that are associated with that individual or institution.

Of key interest here is the obvious role of digital technology as one of the underlying systems in this data-work. As Ozga reminds us, these shifts are not only abstract or discursive, but also intellectual and material. We therefore need to pay close attention to the apparently rational techniques and processes that support these new forms of governance, and question their underlying values and assumptions. In this sense, the digital systems described in this chapter have a number of clear linkages with wider theoretical concerns over the nature and form of contemporary higher education in an era of ongoing 'reformation' and re-casting of the public sector along the lines of 'neoliberal political rationality and business management' (Suspitsyna 2010, p.572). On one hand, this could be seen to involve the displacement of professional power from academic staff to the increased power of managers and administrators (Deem and Brehony 2005). On the other hand, we can clearly identify the rise of discernable new mana-gerial practices that are now prevalent throughout all aspects of the university – from marketing activities, league tables, devolved budgets and targets, systems of self-evaluation, intensified managerial control of curricula, standardized labour processes rigorous imposition of overarching accountability mechanisms, devel-opment planning and performance management, quality assurance and account-ability. These are, as Suspitsyna (2010, p.567) puts it, 'practices that are aimed at controlling and managing educational quality'.

Systems of auditing and surveillance

Much of what has been described in this chapter so far relates to the obviously important role of these digital systems in the production and management of data. Through the continual digital capture, manipulation and representation of data, all these systems could be seen as supporting a data-driven 'audit culture' throughout the university. This links the use of these virtual systems with a range of wider concerns relating to surveillance. We therefore need to consider how the auditing functions of these systems support what could be termed a data-driven 'audit culture' – in particular, the extent to which these practices move beyond the monitoring of individuals (i.e. the automated collection of data) and towards a more implicit system of surveillance where relationships are set up between a control agent and those being monitored (Knox 2010).

As Michael Apple (2010a) observes, the audit culture is a key element of the conservative modernization of education – requiring the constant production of 'evidence' that people within universities are doing things 'efficiently' and in the 'correct' manner. In this sense, institutional technologies (with their emphasis on the digital capture, manipulation and representation of data) could be seen as a key apparatus in the 'active surveillance of people through the documents and databases they produce' (Apple 2010a, p.179). This, then, links the use of institutional technologies such as the VLE, management information system and business decision system with a range of wider concerns over surveillance – most notably Foucauldian concepts of governmentality and disciplinary power. Here, then, the issue of digital technologies such as databases exhibiting panoptic qualities – or in Mark Poster's (1995) terms acting as 'super-panopticons' – raises a range of issues relating to the self-conduct, or in Foucauldian parlance, 'techniques of the self', of individual subjects who regulate their behaviour according to internalized social norms.

Not surprisingly the entrepreneurial rhetoric of a 'bottom-up' individualized empowerment and/or freeing-up of individual action as a result of being engaged within these digital systems is often not readily apparent. That said, these digital systems are often built around a clear individualization, but this is a 'top-down' individualization in terms of the 'disciplinary' character of the LMS or the employment services system. These are systems that are built around what Foucault terms a 'cellular individualization' – involving the observation of a mass of individual academics, administrators, researchers, managers, students and so on; the subsequent hierarchization and judgements made about these individuals; and – most notably – the construction of 'administrative identities' of individuals as 'effective' in their roles. As such, the disciplinary character of these digital systems can be clearly seen in their effects of maximizing the utility as well as the docility of individual bodies (Hoffman 2011). These are systems that are used to make individuals accountable for their actions – primarily in terms of individuals enduring a managerial and bureaucratic accountability to the demands of those at 'higher' levels of management and governance. In this sense, integrated institutional technology systems would seem to be best understood in terms of the replicating the already hierarchic ordering of power and control within the university setting.

Again, this could be argued to be nothing new. After all, universities (as with other large organizations) have long been run along lines of measurement, auditing and comparison. What is significant about these digital systems, however, is

their intensification of an unequal and often undemocratic 'politics of representation'. One example of this is the role of many of these digital systems in extending
the 'politics of representation' within university life – not least in terms of the consequences of how an individual (re)presents themselves online, coupled with what
is also recorded about that individual by others online (Fuery 2009). For example,
one of the main functions of VLEs and workload management systems is to collate
and intensify personal data into publicly accessible profiles. These profiles have the
disempowering effect of displacing people as knowing subjects, and reducing education to a set of digitally based 'textually-mediated work processes' (Daniel 2008,
p.253). This leads to digital systems allowing for the implicit (if not explicit) forms
of 'predictive surveillance' where data relating to past performance and behaviour
is readily available to inform expectations of future behaviours (see Knox 2010).

Crucial here are the ways in which computerized systems allow these data to be
connected, aggregated and used in ways not before possible. For example, online
profiles are often used as a crucial element of the administrative identity of being
an 'effective' or 'deviant' student, teacher or employee – labels that are constructed
'on the basis of knowledge obtained through observation' (Hoffman 2010, p.37)
rather than direct experiences. This 'dataveillance' often functions to decrease the
influence of 'human' experience and judgement, with it no longer seeming to
matter what a tutor may personally know about a student in the face of their 'dash-
board' profile and aggregated tally of positive and negative 'events'. As Bauman
and Lyon (2013) put it, in this manner individuals become wholly defined by their
'data doubles'. As such, there would seem to be little or no room for 'professional'
expertise or interpersonal emotion when faced with such data. In these terms,
institutional technologies could be said to be both dehumanizing *and* deprofes-
sionalizing the relationships between people within a university context.

This turns our attention towards the extent to which these technologies exclude
a range of qualities from the processes and practices of university life. In this
respect, it could also be reasoned that what is *not* represented and known about
within university digital systems is as equally important as what is highlighted and
recorded (Apple 2010b). The silences of these digital systems could be said to be
the more 'difficult' aspects of professionalism, emotions, effort and interpersonal
relationships between the people who 'work' within the university setting. These
issues have little or no space to feature in what is being observed and monitored
when abstracted forms of virtual work are being engaged in. In this way, the operation of VLEs renders what would usually be considered as important aspects of
pedagogic relations unimportant or invisible. For example, in terms of the interpersonal relationships between students and tutors or between groups of administrators and academics, online relationships and interactions might at best take the
form of a 'contrived collegiality' involving coerced collaboration among academics, researchers, managers and administrators (see Grieshaber 2010). These may
not be spontaneous forms of collaborative collegiality, but interactions between
individuals in different roles that are coerced, administratively regulated and orientated around the implementation of pre-determined outcomes.

We therefore need to give thought as to what the consequences of these changes relationships and silences may be. As Murphy (2009, p.684) notes, there are growing concerns that 'fundamental aspects' of educational institutions 'whether they be values, work practices, identities, forms of relation' are being compromised 'under the weight of audit-inspired data'. In interpersonal terms, as well as diminishing the voluntary and spontaneous nature of working relationships, one of the main consequences of these technology-based practices could be said to have been an intensification of mistrust. This is perhaps to be an expected element of any audit culture – as Tatiana Suspitsyna (2010, p.571) concludes:

> The audit culture challenges the grounds of the legitimacy of knowledge and operates on mistrust: the authority of teachers and academics, who are the producers of professional and disciplinary knowledge, is superseded by bureaucratic authority in judging the validity of that knowledge.

Conclusions

In considering the plethora of digital systems underpinning the management and governance of the contemporary university this chapter has developed the argument that these virtual representations of higher education strengthen existing 'top-down' patterns of social power and control through a series of data-driven processes. These systems could therefore be said to function primarily to reinforce an increasingly pervasive 'conservative modernization' of universities – intensifying the managerial control of curricula, the standardization of labour processes and the accountability of educational practices. As such, a number of observations can be made regarding the role of these systems.

Perhaps most prominent is the apparent individualization of practice and action, with all these digital systems appearing to increase the responsibility of the individual in terms of the task of making choices with regards to education, as well as dealing with the consequences of choice. As such, all these systems could be said to demand increased levels of self-dependence and entrepreneurial thinking on the part of the individual, with 'success' in one's work dependent primarily on the individual's ability to self-direct their ongoing digital engagement with university processes and procedures. In this sense, all of the digital systems considered in this chapter could be seen to reinforce many of the individualized behaviours and dispositions that are 'highly valued commodities' within contemporary forms of capitalism – for example, self-directed 'entrepreneurial' behaviour, conviviality and communicative skills, openness, curiosity, reflexivity and so on (see Boltanski and Chiapello 1999/2005). Yet this is not to say that these systems should be associated with any particular individual empowerment or freedom. Instead, these systems are perhaps more accurately described as re-contextualizing higher education along more tightly scripted and restricted lines.

On one hand, these systems could be seen as a new source of tension and conflict between different elements of the university. As Bronwyn Williams (2013, p.174) reasons in relation to the predominance of VLEs and content management systems:

> [T]he adoption and promotion of course management software is driven by material and ideological imperatives of efficiency, control and surveillance that are increasingly central to how the institution of the university works in contemporary culture. The decision to purchase the software illustrates the distinct differences in how the digital university is perceived by administrators, and by many teachers and researchers working with digital media and technologies.

Yet, on the other hand, it could be argued that there is little that could be said to be especially surprising or 'new' about these characteristics and consequences of digital systems in universities. In many ways, these digital systems reinforce the long-standing traditions of being observed, measured and compared in universities (and, indeed, any other work environment). These digital technologies are just another 'management system' that is heavily signified in terms of the traditional roles, regimes and relationships of higher education, and imprinted with power-related agendas and 'scripts' that define appropriate behaviours and interactions. In this way, the primary significance of these digital systems lies in their maintenance and extension of the deeply-held 'value consensus about educational goals' (Ozga 2009, p.153). That said, we should also remain mindful of the 'new' intensifications of inequalities of power and control that appear to be associated with these systems. In this sense, these digital systems could be said to be producing connections between people in universities that either increase power that is authoritative (i.e. dominant authorities getting subordinate others to do what they do not want to do) or else power that is influential (i.e. dominant authorities influencing, shaping or determining the wants and expectations of others).

Thus these digital systems provide a good example of the complex relationships between digital technologies and universities. In many ways, the criticisms raised in this chapter relate to an underlying concern with the ways in which digital technologies remain connected to – rather than separate from – the 'real-life' contexts of higher education. While digital technologies can be imagined as supporting forms of higher education that are more democratic, freer and universally accessible, they can also be seen in contrary terms – 'as a terrifying symbol of control; trails of information, security networks, and so on' (Murphy 2012, p.138). All these concerns suggest that these digital systems act as powerful determinants of human action. These concerns also highlight the need to better recognize the correspondences that persist between digital technology and the real-life social, cultural, economic and political contexts of higher education. With this thought in mind, it is time to turn our attention away from the obviously disembodied manifestations of universities, and towards their decidedly embodied manifestations. How are these issues apparent (if at all) in the work of the contemporary university – not least in the working lives of university staff?

Chapter 4

Digital labour

Digital technology and the working lives of university staff

Introduction

Any analysis of universities is primarily an analysis of people and their work. While not completely absent from our analysis of the digital systems of higher education in Chapter 3, we now need to turn our full attention to those people who work within the context of the university. The digital experiences of students – perhaps the ultimate 'end users' of higher education – will be considered in Chapter 5. For the time being, the present chapter will examine the digitization of higher education from the perspective of those who are employed by universities. This includes university academics, teachers and tutors (groups that are often collectively referred to as 'faculty'), alongside the majority of the higher education workforce – professionals who are variously referred to as university administrators, 'non-faculty' or support staff. Both these sets of workers have seen digital technologies influence substantially the nature of what it is that they do during the course of their professional lives. As such, the digitization of higher education cannot be fully understood without due consideration of the place of digital technology within the working lives, working conditions and working practices of these groups.

Indeed, it is useful to approach technology use as part of the 'work' of university staff. This involves positioning digital technology use within the social and interactional organization of workplace activities, and considering 'the ways in which tools and technologies . . . feature in day-to-day work and collaboration' (Heath et al. 2000, p.299). This approach chimes with our earlier discussions of the changing organizational and institutional nature of the neoliberal university, raising a number of pertinent questions. For example, what is the organization of work and digital technology under neoliberal conditions? What are the processes of digital work and workers' experiences of that work? What tactics and strategies are university workers using in this work? How is this work managed and controlled?

Approaching digital technology along these lines introduces a number of additional shaping influences and issues to our overall analysis of digital higher education. These include the increasingly 'networked' structures of university organization – i.e. the organization of work in ways that are more dispersed and less hierarchical than before. This also includes the recasting of university employees as 'knowledge workers' – increasingly reliant on creative and communicative skills, and flexible and adaptable dispositions. The key concern for this chapter, therefore, is what these changes and shifts actually mean for those people working in universities?

Digital technology and professional 'work' in universities

While many discussions of the 'work' of higher education tend to concentrate on the labour of university academics, teachers and tutors, it is perhaps more useful to first consider these issues in terms of the majority element of the higher education workforce. These are workers variously referred to as 'professional', 'administrative', 'allied' or 'general' staff (although in some institutions, more denigrating labels of 'non-academic', 'non-faculty', 'support' and 'assistant' staff continue to be used). Given the range of skills, autonomy and power that many of these workers now wield within universities, it is most appropriate to refer to these as 'professional' staff. Indeed, reflecting the shift in numbers and power over the past thirty years, Gary Rhoades (2007) goes as far as labelling these staff as 'managerial professionals', in contrast to academics who are now merely 'managed professionals'.

Rhoades' reattribution of power and influence reflects the increased variety of professional staff now working within the contemporary university. For example, a whole industry of 'student services' can now be found in every teaching university – covering functions that range from admissions and financial aid, to careers and academic support. Academic administration of courses and programmes is also a major undertaking, as is dealing with alumni affairs and fund-raising. Institutional research also requires a host of specialized budgeting, accounting and record-keeping positions. Finance, payroll and human relations continue to be major organizational concerns, alongside the management of capital and property. As implied in Chapter 2, the area of 'information services' has understandably grown with respect to computer systems and resources, and altered dramatically with regards to library services. Alongside all of these functions are 'entrepreneurial' concerns such as marketing, business development, public relations and industry liaison. All in all, it is not surprising that professional staff in these areas make up the bulk of the workforce in any university.

Of course, it is important to acknowledge that the umbrella term of 'professional' staff spans a vast range of positions. On one hand are high-status vice-presidents, deputy vice-chancellors and executive directors. Unlike business and commerce, universities have also sustained considerable growth in the numbers of people working in middle-management positions – including directors, executive officers and team leaders. These staff oversee a vast reserve of clerical workers, systems operators, policy officers and technicians – those responsible for executing the bulk of the actual work, rather than its planning and management. Yet despite their number and standing within the day-to-day running of universities, all these professional staff tend to be sidelined in most discussions of higher education. Judy Szekeres (2011) refers to professional staff as 'the invisible workers' within academic discussions of higher education. This applies particularly to the work of university administrators and middle-managers as opposed to the 'managerial elite' responsible for leading university governance. As such, little research has been conducted directly on the working lives of these professional staff and digital technology. However, the studies that have been carried out provide an interesting – but complex – picture.

For many commentators, the role of digital technology for professional staff in universities is analogous to any other modern information and knowledge-orientated organization over the past few decades. One of the most immediate benefits that digital technologies are seen to have brought to university work is supporting new forms of cooperation and collaboration – in particular the flexible and distributed patterns of team work that is now common across university institutions. Unlike the traditional bureaucratic model of isolated divisions and departments, much professional work in universities now involves flexible (and often temporary) project teams. This work is made practically possible through digital technologies that allow shared access to resources, co-authoring and co-editing of materials, group communication and decision-making, and various other forms of real-time and asynchronous collaborative work.

Alongside these digitally-based forms of cooperation and collaboration, digital technologies have altered substantially the nature of communications within universities. In particular, all of the professional roles and functions outlined earlier rely heavily on the use of email – which continues to be perhaps *the* defining work-related technology within universities. In one sense, email is a highly restrictive aspect of university work. As Melonie Fullick (2012) notes, internal communication is a key aspect of the governance of higher education – with tools such as email used in a 'closed, controlled' manner, which reflects the continued dominance with universities of an essentially 'print-dependent' mode of communication. However, in other ways, digital forms of communication such as email could be said to have led to faster communication and less restricted knowledge-sharing practices. The reliance on digital technologies such as desktop computers and smartphones is also seen to allow professional staff a degree of latitude to combine work and personal activities. In this latter sense, it has been suggested that digital technologies have led to a number of individual benefits. These include flexible working practices, spaces for employees to share employment and career-related knowledge, opportunities to pursue personal interests, new spaces for self-organized employee resistance and even union revitalization (Richards 2012). From this perspective, digital technology is seen by some commentators to benefit the individual worker as well as their employing institutions.

The messy realities of digital technology and professional 'work' in universities

These potential benefits may ring true for some professional staff, but do not reflect the rather more complicated realities of working with digital technology. Take for example, the changing nature of professional functions and roles. As shall be discussed in more detail in Chapter 6, automated book self-issue/return machines have now taken the place of many counter staff in university libraries – thus supporting 'a more human' library experience as the marketing campaign of one manufacturer of such machines puts it (3M 2007). Similar automation and replacement of roles has occurred with reception staff in university departments and faculties – with video conferencing systems and automated entry systems now allowing an individual receptionist to cover multiple locations on a virtual rather than face-to-face basis. Other functions and roles have been virtually 'outsourced' to commercial contractors and suppliers – from data entry and transcription to accounting and marketing. As discussed in Chapter 3, many other professional functions are now mediated through computerized online systems – such as dealing with human resources, finance teams and so on. In many universities, it is expected that a student or academic can fulfil all of the administrative requirements of their university through virtual portals, online proformas and email. Of course, these tasks still involve behind-the-scenes human involvement, yet this takes place at a distance and on an asynchronous basis. A librarian still has to retrieve the returned books and relocate them on the shelves. A finance officer still has to approve and process the expense claim forms. These are not roles that have been completely automated, although the nature of the work (and therefore the professional role) has clearly shifted.

The increased presence of digital technologies in professional higher education work is therefore bound with the changing nature of universities as workplaces. On the one hand, the establishment of the managerial, neoliberal model of the university outlined in earlier chapters has certainly involved the technology-supported expansion of some areas of professional work. For example, the increased important of data and information has given rise to a new cadre of information officers, systems developers and data analysts. Whole teams of professionals are now responsible for workload management systems, student databases, finance systems, and research application and auditing systems. The crucial issue here is how these digital systems now mediate much of the work of these professional staff, thus further contributing to 'invisibility of their work' (Allen-Collinson 2007). On the other hand, staff working in these roles have become identified more closely with the managerial practices associated with these technologies – further contributing to the 'fragility of relationships' between academic and professional staff (Szekeres 2011). With digital systems now used to facilitate and embody governance regulations, accountability and reporting functions, face-to-face contact between administrators and academics now increasingly takes place only when there has been a problem within the usually automated system. These digital systems therefore further the 'academic apartheid' between university staff – adding to academic perceptions of professional staff as 'agents of external forces in a culture of compliance' (McNay 2005, p.41), or 'the bearers of much that is wrong with the academy, e.g. bureaucratization, economization and management by documents' (Gillberg 2010, p.132).

A further set of more personal issues is raised in Melissa Gregg's (2011) study of the role of digital technology and media in the working lives of middle-class office professionals. Gregg examined the experiences of university administrators (and academics), alongside people working in broadcast media, cultural organizations and marketing companies. Tellingly, the technology-based working conditions and practices that have been established across these sectors were remarkably similar, leading to the general conclusion that 'new media technology encourages and exacerbates a much older tendency among salaried professional to put work at the heart of daily concerns, often at the expense of all other sources of intimacy and fulfillment' (Gregg 2011, p.xi).

Gregg associated the use of digital technology with two insidious trends in the work of university administrators – what she termed 'presence bleed' and 'function creep'. By 'presence bleed' Gregg was referring to the dissolving of once firm boundaries between work and home, and between professional and personal identities. Digital technology – not least laptop computers, mobile phones, remote access to email systems and work files – was permitting professional staff to cope with expanding workloads by working at weekends, evenings and early mornings. As Gregg (2011, p.1) put it, university work 'has broken out of the office into cafes, trains, streets, dining rooms and bedroom'. Tellingly, this was the case not just for the high-flying executive directors and managers, but for those professional staff working in much 'more mundane' administrative positions and roles (p.2). One of the most common forms that this 'presence bleed' took was the practice of late-evening and early-morning maintenance of work email accounts. This was described throughout Gregg's interviews as not checking email per se, but simply deleting emails in an effort to be mentally prepared for going to work. Tellingly, nearly all of Gregg's respondents did not see this as 'work'.

Gregg's identification of the 'function creep' associated with digital technology was perhaps more subtle – pointing to the role of technology in obscuring the amount of additional work, responsibilities and remit that professional staff are being given. Despite the veneer of team work and group collegiality within organizations, Gregg highlights the intensification and individualization of university professional work through digital technology – with individuals being publically assigned specific responsibility for tasks. Again, the (mis)use of email was raised as particularly prevalent. Another common issue raised by many interviewees in Gregg's study was the inappropriate use of multiple emailing – what could be termed the tyranny of the 'cc' and 'bcc' functions that allow multiple people to be 'copied in' to an email message. These practices were a common source of intensifying the work of professional staff, with email being used to 'pass on' or 'devolve down' responsibility for work, or copying in bosses to accelerate power plays or bring conflicts to a head.

Gregg's study therefore highlights a number of usually unacknowledged consequences of the digitization of professional work within the university. First is the increased exploitation of professional workers through a digitally-mediated pressure to over-work. These pressures can take different forms according to workers' positions. For example, Gregg found senior staff and middle-managers working on discrete projects having to intensify their computer-based home work as project deadlines approached – working long hours (and occasionally whole-night sessions). These intense periods of works were not seen as abnormal, but rather part of the rhythm of project work. Often these were not accidental oversights, but had been planned explicitly into initial project proposals. Conversely, lower-status staff were subject to an underlying constant sense of surveillance through the publically visible online calendars, unread emails and other digital records. This sense of surveillance was felt to involve supervisors and colleagues and team members. These pressures, Gregg found, were intensified for professional staff working at the periphery of the organization – on fractional contracts or in job-shares, where the university authorities can claim that other people need to have access to 'personal' email accounts and computer files. Indeed, dealing with email was reported to be an important part of being seen to be an effective 'team player'. For example, this pressure was experienced acutely by professional staff dealing with students emailing outside of traditional 'office hours', and expecting swift responses. Again part-time, casual and sessional staff reported feeling an intensified 'pressure to maintain the communication standards of full-time colleagues' (Gregg 2011, p.59).

Gregg's study highlighted powerfully the emotional and human consequences of these working conditions and working practices. Running throughout her study is a sense of depersonalization of university work. On one hand, digital technology could be seen as a space for resistance at work. The mediation of one's working life through a desktop computer could be seen as an opportunity for what is sometimes termed 'cyber loafing' – i.e. sending personal emails, using social networks such as Facebook, playing games or online shopping (Kellaway 2013). This is evident in the trend amongst some university staff to take their lunch 'al-desko' in front of the screen rather than outside of the office. On the other hand, as Gregg (2011, p.60) points out, all these 'personal' acts take place through the IT system that provides the 'main "face" of the [university] organization – a point of access and address'. As such, even these temporary digital pleasures offer little solace from work.

Another key point from Gregg's analysis is the obviously gendered nature of these trends for a profession that contains a majority of female workers. While female and male workers suffered from missing out on leisure pursuits, personal relationships, home and family commitments, Gregg's study highlighted strongly gendered assumptions behind the long-hours, weekend-working culture now associated with digital technology use. In particular, Gregg noted how the consequences of being only 'partially present' at home were exacerbated for women with families, or those women in relationships where there was no reduction in the household division of labour. For these women, at-home university work was not replacing domestic work, but merely adding to it.

Digital technology and academic 'work' in universities

We should now turn our attention towards the place of digital technology within the working lives of university faculty. On the one hand, digital technologies are now integral elements of the core functions of a university academic – be it teaching, research, public engagement or private scholarship. For instance, digital technologies have had a profound effect on the processes and practices of academic research – from the generation and collection of data; the ways in which data are 'mined', organized, stored analysed and represented; the ways in which research findings are communicated; as well as the collaboration of different researchers around the world. As Pfeffer (2012, p.167) observes, 'no researcher today can do without at least some basic form of computing'.

On the other hand, most of the more mundane issues relating to professional work just outlined in the previous section of this chapter apply equally to university academics. The past thirty years have seen a notable digital displacement of administrative and clerical work from professional staff to academic staff (not least in terms of word-processing, email, diary maintenance and so on). As such, many academics are also subject to the 'presence bleed' and 'function creep' described earlier. Thus for university academics (i.e. 'faculty' or the 'professoriate'), digital technology is certainly perceived as a double-edged sword. Indeed, Schuster and Finkelstein (2006) described digital technology as a 'wild card' in the traditionally ordered world of the university professor – threatening to transform fundamentally the nature of academic work. Regardless of whether one sees this transformation along improved or diminished lines, digital technologies are certainly now an integral feature of the daily working lives of every academic. For instance, most (if not all) of this long list of practices are now familiar parts of the modern academic working life in ways that they would not have been a decade or so before:

- communicating through email, mobile telephone, video conference and voice over internet protocol (VOIP) applications such as Skype;
- writing with word-processors, as well as through blogs and microblogs;
- reading online journals and e-books;
- managing teaching though LMSs, MOOCs and other forms of online education;
- using and creating teaching resources with digital video, digital audio and other content-creation packages;
- assessing students' work through e-marking applications, plagiarism detection software and entering grades into databases and management information systems;

- managing research – from applications to end-of-project reports – through research management systems;
- using computers to gather, store and analyse research data;
- disseminating research and writing through official university web pages, social networking sites, online journals and other forms of e-publishing;
- managing time (and having one's time managed) through shared online calendars;
- recording and evidencing work through time sheets and workload management systems.

Lurking beneath these continuous flows of digital work, however, are questions of what relationships now exist between such technological practices and the (re)organization of academic work. For example, to what extent are these technologies fitting around and facilitating existing patterns and forms of academic work? Are these technologies supporting new forms of academic work? What are the consequences (both intended and unintended) of these digital practices for university academics? As has been the case with most issues so far in this book, these relatively simple questions belie a host of rather more complex issues.

The potential benefits of digital technology in the work of university academics – towards the 'digital scholar'?

On one hand, many commentators contend that digital technologies are a largely beneficial element of the working practices and working conditions of the contemporary academic. As such – so the argument goes – university faculty are beholden to make extensive and effective use of digital technology. This is certainly the argument pursued by Martin Weller – professor of educational technology at the UK's Open University, and therefore positioned at the forefront of such things. Like many others in the academic educational technology community, Weller is convinced of the centrality of digital technology and digital media to the efficient functioning of university academics in the twenty-first century. This is laid out in his unequivocally titled book, *The digital scholar: how technology is transforming digital practice*. Here, Weller is not simply concerned with the use of word-processing, PowerPoint, VLEs, email and the other established everyday tools of working in university environments. Indeed, he describes these digital practices as a 'business as usual model' that is not 'worthy of particular interest' (2011, p.6). Instead Weller's enthusiasm stems from the 'substantial change in scholarly practice' (p.6) that is induced by the ways-of-doing and ways-of-being associated with recent digital developments such as social media. This change is reflected in this book itself – written over a four-year period by blogging, tweeting, social bookmarking and 'remotely' attending seminars and conferences. Extrapolating these shifts in the practice of his academic writing to other areas of scholarly activity such as teaching, research and public engagement, Weller develops a persuasive case for digital technologies altering fundamentally what academics do, and how they do it.

The changing nature of academic work, Weller argues, is associated with three shifts in digital practice: the nature of digital content, the role of the social network, and open models of interaction and access. First and foremost is that fact that increasing amounts of academic work is now networked. This contrasts sharply with the scholarly practices of the twentieth century and before, which were shaped by the analogue systems that they took place within – i.e. academic libraries, print-based publishing, face-to-face conferences, seminars and courses. These, Weller contends, were all systems built around the notion of 'high thresholds' to accessing knowledge. Now with networked digital technologies there are far fewer thresholds, meaning that scholarly practices can change to suit these new conditions. Key here are practices of 'sharing' and 'openness' – which Weller sees both as technical features of new digital technologies but also as a 'state of mind' for the people who are using them (p.7). These practices are likely to alter the landscape of academic work – a point that Weller expands through consideration of Ernest Boyer's (1990) four elements of scholarship – i.e. 'discovery' (creation of new knowledge, research); 'integration' (interpretation and interdisciplinary work, making connections and placing one's work in the wider context); 'application' (engagement with the wider world); and 'teaching'.

For example, in terms of the changing nature of scholarly 'discovery' and academic research, Weller argues that it is the combination of digital data and 'the global network that is really beginning to alter research practice' (p.45). Scholars now engage in what Weller terms a 'networked research cycle' – commencing with the development of initial ideas through to the eventual dissemination of their findings. Weller marvels at the research potential of 'grid' technologies (combining lots of different computers) and 'crowd sourcing' (combining lots of individual minds) on specific research problems. He also highlights the benefits of taking an open, collaborative approach to the data collection and analysis processes of academic research – with digital technologies allowing global practices of data sharing and data visualization. This, Weller reasons, can only lead to quicker and better academic research, with open access and widespread sharing leading to more thorough and sustained forms of scrutiny and continuous peer review, as well as fairer and wider dissemination.

Seen from this perspective, academic research is a more socialized and more social endeavour. Through digital technology, the research community is no longer confined to the institution in which one works, and the conferences that one can attend. Weller talks in enthusiastic terms of his own personal networks of thousands of different contacts, arguing that for his academic work Twitter operates as 'an interdisciplinary network' par excellence. These developments are perhaps most noticeable in the changing nature of the traditionally stuffy and staid academic conference cycle. Now academic conferences are notable for the high numbers of people participating remotely, the 'backchannel' of conversation that takes place on platforms such as Twitter, the alternative session formats (such as 'un-conferences', 'teach-meets' and so on), and the offline social events where already digitally-connected collegial groups gather to meet on a rare face-to-face basis. For less technology-savvy attendees, much of what now takes place at an academic conference must certainly be a bewildering experience.

These shifts in the 'work' of academic research notwithstanding, Weller singles out university teaching for perhaps to largest changes to have taken place. As he puts it, 'teaching [is] where we see the biggest impact of digital resources and open approaches. The digitization of learning and teaching resources means that they are easily reproducible and sharable at a global scale' (p.49). Weller's argument here is that teaching and learning now take place in a qualitatively and quantitatively different landscape, where content and expert knowledge is available freely and easily accessed and shared. Students no longer have to learn from one expert teacher, but from a variety of networked resources – engaging in user-driven forms of discovery and problem-based learning. Teaching is no longer a case of expert-led instruction, but supporting individuals to learn how to make connections, develop the capacity to know more, nurture and maintain connections to support continual learning, and being able to choose what is best to learn at any particular time. Within these conditions, university teachers now have to engage in what Weller terms a 'pedagogy of abundance' (p.85) – teaching in networked, open ways that mirror the nature of the resources and the ways of learning that digital technologies support. Citing the examples of 'open education resources' and 'open courses', Weller reasons that digital technology has turned many of the traditional assumptions of teaching on their head – i.e. that teaching talent is scarce, that locating good teaching talent is difficult, that content must be physical, that content is manufactured to demand, and that access to content is scarce (p.85).

For Weller, then, the contemporary academic should be willing to work in ways that are networked and open. The 'digital scholar' is well connected, always curious, with a 'default' predilection to share over a range of informal and formal channels. Crucially, digital technology demands a personalization of academic work – Weller argues that academics need to be willing to mix their professional and personal lives, as the personal elements of one's life act as 'hooks through which [professional] connections are made' (p.100). In contrast to what has long been seen as the traditional roles of the university academic (i.e. research, application, integration and teaching), Weller suggests that they are now 'engagement', 'experimentation', 'reflection' and 'sharing' (p.184). This is not to say that the traditional structures and conventions of academe are now defunct or have no place, but that they are being complemented and often usurped by these alternative digital practices. As Weller (p.184) concludes:

> [T]his is a period of transition for scholarship, as significant as any other in its history, from the founding of universities to the establishment of peer review and the scientific methods. It is also a period that holds tension and even some paradoxes: it is both business as usual and yet a time of considerable change.

The potential diminishment of university academics – towards a 'digital deskilling'?

Of course, there are plenty of reasons to remain suspicious of such enthusiastically certain accounts. A sizable body of writing and commentary has argued to the contrary of Weller's portrayal of the 'digital scholar' – pointing instead to the fundamentally divisive ways that digital technologies actually act to impinge on the lives and freedoms of academic workers. Much of this discontent is associated with a loss of professional freedoms as university authorities and bureaucracies use digital technologies to organize, rationalize and ultimately control the work of academics. There are certainly many clumsy examples within higher education of digital technologies being used in this way. For example, as discussed in Chapter 3, academics submitting research proposals to funding councils are routinely coerced into writing certain numbers of words, using standardized fonts and sizes, and generally conforming to arbitrary presentational rules. Conversely, when a member of teaching staff leaves a university department, their modules and courses continue to be taught using their teaching resources, course notes and (most importantly) their PowerPoint slides – all which are retained in the university learning management system. One particularly ill-judged use of digital technology was the case at the beginning of 2013, when the University of Warwick hastily withdrew its leaked plans to monitor the daily whereabouts of 'overseas' staff members through their email accounts in an attempt to satisfy the concerns of UK immigration authorities.

Intrusive and demeaning as these practices might be, we need to consider further what consequences they might have for academic work, and the role of the university academic. One often-cited argument is that digital technologies act to fragment and 'unbundle' the constituent elements of the academic role. Thus, through digital technologies, the processes of selecting and admitting students into a university, looking after their pastoral needs, assessing their work and supporting their selection of courses can all be outsourced to different people. Various elements of what used to be seen as an academic's personal responsibility can be devolved to other professional groups, such as assessment specialists, counsellors, website developers and instructional designers. These trends have clear resonances with the Marxist analysis of the deskilling of assembly workers on the factory-line – with the conception and execution of tasks separated and automated through tools to the extent that craft-like work that was once the domain of highly-skilled specialists can be performed by much lower-skilled workers (see Braverman 1974). In this sense, as Smith and Rhoades (2006) put it, digital technologies can be seen as a 'virtual assembly line' for university academics.

The argument therefore persists that digital technology is a tool by which university administrations control the conditions of academic work. This was the general thrust of a popular article (later extended into a book) by the historian David Noble titled 'Digital diploma mills' (1998). Here, Noble presented a deliberate updating of Robert Reid's classic 1959 study of the post-war US expansion of 'diploma mills' – massified forms of education provider, which Reid described as typified by having 'no classrooms', teaching staff who were 'often untrained or nonexistent' and administrators and officers who were 'unethical self-seekers whose qualifications are no better than their offerings' (1998, n.p.). In Noble's eyes, the rapid integration of digital technologies into the teaching regimes of universities at the end of the 1990s was cause for similar concern. Noble's concern was prompted by North American universities such as UCLA and Toronto's York University introducing mandatory use of websites for all of their courses, while at the same time setting up for-profit companies to sell online education. For the critical-minded commentator such as Noble, these activities constituted clear battle-lines. On the one side were 'university administrators and their myriad commercial partners', on the other side 'those who constitute the core relation of education: students and teachers' (n.p.).

While clearly peddling his own political agenda, Noble's prognosis of the e-learning boom of the late 1990s and early 2000s remains compelling and concerning. For Noble, these developments involved at least five different groups. On one hand, were student and faculty – kept largely 'in the dark' and not involved in decision-making processes or consulted about the technological changes to their courses and working conditions. On the other hand, were IT industry 'vendors' keen to sell computer hardware, network infrastructure, software and 'content'. The values of this latter group were endorsed by 'corporate training advocates' and the 'educational technology' lobby of academics and enthusiasts (who Noble dismissively describes as 'ubiquitous technozealots who simply view computers as the panacea for everything, because they like to play with them' (n.p.)). Finally – and most significant in Noble's mind – were university authorities and administrators

> who see it as a way of giving their institutions a fashionably forward–looking image. More importantly, they view computer–based instruction as a means of reducing their direct labor and plant maintenance costs – fewer teachers and classrooms – while at the same time undermining the autonomy and independence of faculty. At the same time, they are hoping to get a piece of the commercial action for their institutions or themselves, as vendors in their own right of software and content.
>
> (Noble 1998, n.p.)

In highlighting what he described as the 'overriding commercial intent and market orientation behind these initiatives' (n.p.), Noble's analysis echoes what was described in Chapter 2 regarding the commodification of the neoliberal university. Yet this description is perhaps most useful in extenuating the consequences of this digitally-based commercialization and commodification of university teaching and learning for the university staff who are compelled to enact it.

As Noble describes it, the use of digital technology by academic staff is the direct consequence of the first step in the commercialization of higher education, which saw the rapid expansion of university students (in the role of customers) alongside the introduction of increased tuition fees (in the form of profits). This led almost inevitably to a situation where existing university infrastructures and modes of delivery were tested to breaking point – as Noble puts it 'campuses were in crisis'. At this point, Noble reasons, 'the commercialization of academia and commoditization of instruction' – primarily along digital lines – 'is touted as the solution to the crisis engendered by the first' (n.p.). One of Noble's chief contentions is that this logic vastly overestimates the transformative qualities of digital technology. Technology, he argues, is simply not capable of 'increasing the efficiencies of already overextended teachers' (n.p.). In fact, he reasons that technology-based teaching generally involves more instructor time and effort, and increased direct and overhead costs than 'traditional' methods. As a means of efficiency and streamlining the 'business' of university teaching, therefore, these 'high-tech remedies are bound only to compound the problem' (n.p.).

Noble's thesis is perhaps most useful in its recognition of the fundamental alternations to the nature and form of academic teaching and teachers implicit in these organizational adjustments. Under a regime of instruction based around the delivery of digital content, Noble saw teachers as labour becoming primarily content producers, and hence 'subject to all the pressures that have befallen production workers in other industries undergoing rapid technological transformation from above' (n.p.). By this Noble was highlighting the implicit digitally-led 'deskilling', disciplining and ultimate displacement of university teachers, akin to any skilled worker whose craft is automated. First was the restructuring and fragmentation of the teaching process into constituent elements of content creation, instructional design, delivery of instructional content and eventual assessment. As Noble pointed out, once original teaching content has been created, then all the other stages of this production line can be either automated or carried out by a less-skilled person in a classic Taylorist fashion. Noble describes this restructuring as therefore reducing the autonomy, independence and control that university faculty have over their work, ultimately implying their 'long-term redundancy'. As Noble put it, 'once the faculty converts its courses to courseware, their services are in the long run no longer required' (n.p.). More subtly, the technology also introduces a new class of 'teaching technician' who is responsible for the second-hand (re)presentation of instructional materials, but shorn of any connection to its production. These developments, Noble argues, were classic examples of the use of technology by management primarily as a means of exploitation of labour:

> Once faculty put their course material online, moreover, the knowledge and course design skill embodied in that material is taken out of their possession, transferred to the machinery and placed in the hands of the administration. The administration is now in a position to hire less skilled, and hence cheaper, workers to deliver the technologically pre-packaged course. It also allows the administration, which claims ownership of this commodity, to peddle the course elsewhere without the original designer's involvement or even

knowledge, much less financial interest. The buyers of this packaged com-modity, meanwhile, other academic institutions, are able thereby to contract out, and hence outsource, the work of their own employees and thus reduce their reliance upon their in-house teaching staff.

(Noble 1998, n.p.)

Noble saw these developments as largely unavoidable. He saw university staff as in little position to resist – with most staff left in a position where they can engage with digital technology either 'dutifully or grudgingly (it doesn't really matter which)' (n.p.). Those 'skeptical faculty' who would like to assume that their unique and expert contribution to teaching could not be automated and mechanically replicated 'will be automated anyway' as the pursuit of profit out-weighs any concern with educational quality. Significantly, Noble saw the great-est pressures to comply with these developments as being placed on the 'most vulnerable' groups in the academic workforce – i.e. 'untenured and part–time faculty, and entry-level and prospective employees'. Noble (n.p.) therefore ended his analysis on a suitably bleak note:

> [A] dismal new era of higher education has dawned. In ten years, we will look upon the wired remains of our once great democratic higher education system and wonder how we let it happen. That is, unless we decide now not to let it happen.

Looking to the realities of working with digital technology

While Noble's diagnosis may well chime with the personal politics of some read-ers of this book, it needs to be seen as deliberately exaggerated and polemic as Weller's previous enthusiastic endorsement of digital academic labour. As has been repeated throughout all of the chapters so far, there is a need to remain circumspect and realistic in our analysis of digital technology and education if we are to avoid excessively doomster or boomster perspectives. Digital technol-ogy certainly can become an emotive area of academic discussion. A usefully bal-anced counterpoint to these two visions of the empowered digital scholar or the deskilled digital dupe is offered by a recent study by David R. Johnson of the University of Georgia. The starting point for this study was the contention that if new technologies really are contributing to the erosion of professional control in the ways just described, then many academics would be actively resisting and rejecting their use. Indeed, as was noted at the beginning of Chapter 1, academ-ics are a generally disgruntled and strong-willed group of professionals who need little encouragement to disengage or be uncooperative. It would seem unlikely that academics would give much time to any imposed work practice that they per-ceive as wholly illegitimate or ineffective, or contribute willingly to circumstances associated with the loss of control over their conditions of work. Thus the fact that so many academics make sustained use of what could be seen as oppressive digital technologies clearly merits further consideration. Johnson's study therefore focuses on the meanings that faculty attached to the use of digital technologies for their teaching, therefore shedding light on the context of digitally-based work 'as it is experienced and seen through the eyes of those exposed to pressures for technological change' (2013, p.131).

Based on in-depth interviews with forty-two 'professors' (in the North American sense of academic tutors and teachers) working within anthropology, biology, chemistry and engineering departments at three high-status universities in the US, Johnson's study contains some revealing findings. First, very few academics were found to be using 'teaching and learning' technologies for overtly pedagogic reasons. Instead, professors were more commonly motivated by the gains derived from enhanced visualization of content in forms that could then be readily stored, and later distributed to students. Often these visual technologies (most commonly handouts, PowerPoint slides, video clips and the like) were being used as pragmatic means of coping with ever-larger classes of students. The in-class use of these tools was also often intended to attract students' attention, and motivate them to remain engaged with the course. Crucially, faculty were often using technology in their teaching despite deeply-held reservations regarding the pedagogic benefits of doing so. As Johnson (p.135) reported:

> Not only did professors perceive new technologies as of limited value, many viewed technologically rich instruction as detrimental to student learning. They believe that students view course management software, presentation software, and the Internet as substitutes for learning. Technology as a substitute takes two forms. The most common view is that technology rich classes relieve students of the need to attend . . . Professors also believe technology presents a problem for learning when students perceive it as a substitute for understanding the fundamental components of analysis.

So how did it come to be like this? Johnson's research implies a situation that is more complex than the straightforward deskilling of all academics, and certainly does not suggest any notion of empowered 'digital scholarship'. Instead, these findings conveyed a distinct clash between the imposition of teaching technologies by university authorities and the working lives and labour conditions of university teachers. On one hand, then, Johnson's interviewees (p.138) were clearly responding to the symbolic and 'ceremonial' nature of instructional technology:

> where 'razzle-dazzle' technology becomes a prop in a dramatic enactment of the socially constructed notion that legitimate universities are on the 'cutting edge' of technology . . . communicat[ing] legitimacy to external audiences, such as parents, students, and prospective employers of university graduates.

Yet, crucially, on the other hand, there appeared to be little or no sense of academics having been consulted about the procurement of their universities' instructional technologies and tools. Thus the 'need' to use digital technologies for teaching was manufactured through the unsolicited establishment of technology-rich teaching and learning environments (i.e. the centralized purchasing of LMSs, technology-laden lecture theatres and so on) coupled with the concurrent enrolment of even larger classes and student cohorts. As such, it is unsurprising that all but a handful of Johnson's interviewees were using technology to ease the burden of teaching large class sizes and to sustain students' attention and good-will.

A telling aspect of Johnson's analysis was his observation that some academics were able to resist and reject the worst of these pressures, while others were coerced into technology use despite their pedagogic concerns – thereby significantly undermining professional expertise and professional autonomy. Those faculty who were in the privileged position of being able to work around the pressures to employ digital teaching techniques tended to be those who saw themselves as research active, and accordingly directed their efforts towards the generally research-focused academic reward system. Tellingly, these absenters were usually higher-ranked members of staff who were in a position to 'protect' the time required to be a 'productive researcher'. From this privileged position, the diminishing returns of spending time engaging with new instructional technologies were easily justified. Conversely, those members of staff who appeared to have 'chosen' to make 'innovative' use of technology in their teaching, often tended to be either on lower-status 'teaching-track' career paths, or with regular appointments but having less established research careers. Either way, using educational technology was perceived by all groups to be a lesser option to that of engaging in academic research. Those faculty who were using digital technologies (albeit reluctantly and against their better judgement) were therefore being disadvantaged in a number of ways.

Johnson's analysis therefore reverses the logic of the usually stated 'problem' of academic staff and digital technology. In other words, the 'problem' may not be that some academics make little or no use of technology in their teaching, but that so many academics are feeling compelled to do so. This study certainly highlights a disjuncture that persists between what university authorities are trying to encourage university academics to do with digital technology, and what many faculty members feel is appropriate. As such, academics' use of digital technology is as much as site of struggle as it is for the administrative, professional and support staff discussed earlier. In the case of Johnson's university faculty, these struggles centred on issues of academic freedom, professional autonomy, pedagogic beliefs and the primacy of research, writing and personal scholarship over other aspects of work. The key point here, however, is that while some academics have the occupational status and power to circumvent such pressures, others do not. Those who are unable to resist the pressures of technology-based teaching can only stand passively by as an 'unbundling' of their work takes place.

Of course, it is important to reiterate the differentiation of this process. As Johnson puts it, rather than all faculty being passive objects of technological deskilling, 'academe's status as a profession [is] a source of influence in technological change' (p.144). Unfortunately it appears that only those faculty in relatively powerful and privileged positions can resist the worst impositions of digital technology onto their working lives and professional identities. As such, inequalities are forming between those who enjoy high-status careers in research and graduate studies and those who are left using technology to wrangle large undergraduate classes. Inevitably, these divisions in academic status are notably divided in terms of gender, class, ethnicity and so on. In UK universities, for example, whereas 44 per cent of academics are female, this falls to 19 per cent of tenured full professors. Similar disproportions exist for ethnic minority and disabled staff. Thus the use and non-use of digital technology is entwined with the wider disparities and inequalities of academic labour. Far from being a democratic 'leveller', digital technology could well be seen as part of the problem of academic workplace inequalities, rather than part of any solution.

Conclusions

This chapter has addressed the use of digital technologies within the working environment of the contemporary university. By approaching digital education from this perspective of organizational labour, a number of important issues are brought to the fore. These include the potential of digital technology to lead to the empowerment or exploitation of university workers. For example, we have seen how digital technologies are implicated within the various divisions of labour faced by professional and academic workers – i.e. the 'stream of differentiated and discrete tasks' that workers are expected to deal with (Randall et al. 2007, p.235). Digital technologies are implicit in the distribution of tasks and their distribution to others – as well as their dispersal into what would have traditionally been seen as non-work environments. Indeed, digital technologies appear associated closely with the establishment of university work as 'social factory' – i.e. the expansion of work beyond the places where the production process traditionally takes place (such as the factory or the office) into the places of wider society (such as the home and local community) (Tronti 2012). For many university workers, then, it increasingly is irrelevant to talk of 'home' as distinct from 'university', or 'work' as distinct from 'life'. Society is now an extension of the workplace, and the controls that are associated with it. As Guy Standing (2011, p.38) concludes: '[T]he flexibility involves more work-for-labour, a blurring of workplaces, home places and public places; and a shift from direct control to diverse forms of indirect control, in which increasingly sophisticated technological mechanisms are deployed.'

This chapter has also demonstrated how the planned 'impacts' and prescribed 'consequences' of digital technology systems come up against the 'immediate context of conduct' of technology use *in situ* (Suchman 1987). Thus these are workplace technologies that are dependent upon the circumstances in which they are invoked. In other words, these are technologies that do not uniformly deter-mine conduct 'but rather provide a resource through which individuals organize their own actions and interpret the conduct of others' (Heath et al. 2000, p.303). A key point here, then, are the meanings that university workers attach to digital technologies – i.e. how particular groups 'ascribe, dispute, exclude and cohere the sense and significance of objects and artifacts' (Heath et al. 2000, p.305).

Obviously, these issues and consequences should not be portrayed in a wholly negative light. Digital technologies clearly benefit some university workers, while disadvantaging others. As Barley and Kunda (2001, p.79) reason:

> A number of theorists have tied the emergence of new forms of organizing to the spread of digital technologies which are said to undermine job struc-tures, increase the complexity of production processes, and require a more highly skilled workforce. Others have argued equally forcefully that technol-ogy engenders precisely the opposite developments. More grounded studies indicate, however, that digital technologies are used in a variety of ways and have a variety of effects on the way firms organize. They can automate or informate work, they can create or eliminate jobs, they can deskill, enskill, or reskill work, and more often than we think, they may occasion no change all. Thus, whether and how a digital technology affects the way an organiza-tion is structured depends on how the technology is designed, the way it is deployed, and how it is used and interpreted in a specific organizational context.

This is an admirably balanced perspective, and undoubtedly reflects the complex relationship between university work and digital technology. However, it would seem from the evidence reviewed in this chapter that digital technologies appear likely to be having a detrimental impact on those workers who are in more periph-eral and more vulnerable positions. These are the teachers who are coerced and compelled to engage in online instruction to the detriment of their professional autonomy, as opposed to the research professors who can circumvent the worst excesses. These are the professional staff working on part-time, job-share and/or temporary arrangements, whose work is monitored through online systems, or the working mothers who are compelled to maintain the same (over)working patterns in the office and at home as their less burdened colleagues. In all these respects, digital technologies do not appear to be leading to a more level playing field, or less hierarchized working environment. On the contrary, the ongoing digitization of university work seems to be having a worse effect on those in the most vulnerable and 'precarious' roles. A key question to take forward from this chapter is what (if anything) can university workers do about this situation, and who outside of higher education would care? As Langdon Winner noted gloomily at the beginning of the integration of digital technology into the mainstream of university life:

[M]ost faculty of college and universities now seem unaware of or indifferent to changes planned for the ways of working in the years ahead . . . If professions ever do begin to squawk about the erosion of their scholarly autonomy, the general public probably won't care.

(Winner 1998, p.337)

Chapter 5

Digital study

Digital technology and the 'student experience'

Introduction

As part of our analysis of digital technology as 'labour' within higher education, we also need to consider the working lives of the students who fill university courses and campuses. The massification referred to throughout this book has seen a diversification of the type of 'student' now studying in one form or another at university. Most universities now have extensive 'pre-degree', 'pre-sessional' and 'foundation' programmes – catering for prospective undergraduate students who lack the necessary entry qualifications. These feed into the vast undergraduate programmes themselves – delivered in full-time and part-time 'modes', face-to-face and at a distance, throughout daytimes and evenings, on weekdays and at weekends. Most universities offer a variety of post-graduate professional programmes – from teacher training and counselling, to medical, health and business specializations. There are also many academic postgraduate taught programmes, with students studying for master's degrees and professional doctorates in a variety of forms, modes and timings. Alongside all this activity are students engaged in higher degrees – master's degrees by research, doctoral research and other forms of advanced study. All in all, universities are host to a variety of 'teaching provision' and, therefore, types of student and varieties of 'student experience'.

Given their prevalence within higher education settings, students remain curiously overlooked in many discussions of educational technology. As the ultimate 'end users' of much of the digital technologies discussed so far in this book, it is telling that consideration of student-focused technologies tend to be concerned actually with issues relating to teachers and technology. Many commentators appear happy to assume that students are a relatively unproblematic variable within the educational technology equation. Most students – especially those entering university directly from compulsory schooling – are assumed to come from age cohorts that are fully up to speed with digital technology, and therefore willing and able to use it during their studies. Thus while these students may present a 'problem' in terms of their increasing expectations of digital higher education, they tend to be seen as a non-critical element of technology use in universities.

To overlook students in the way, of course, misses some of the most significant issues that shape the use of digital technology in higher education. As this chapter will now go on to discuss, students' experiences of – and engagements with – digital technology during their university careers are as complex, compromised and problematic as those of academic and professional staff. Indeed, the 'work' of being a university student has a significant influence on the shaping of digital higher education. As such, the experiences of students need to be given due consideration if we are to develop a full understanding of digital technology within contemporary higher education.

The university student as 'digital native' – a mistaken identity?

We first need to re-consider the general assumptions that many people have about the cohorts of students currently studying within universities. Here, the received wisdom tends to be that university students – as predominantly young, well-educated and well-resourced individuals – are inclined inherently towards using digital technologies within their day-to-day lives and, it follows, are well-disposed towards academic use of technology. Indeed, present cohorts of undergraduate students are seen to be drawn from the generation of 'digital natives' who grew up with the internet during the 1990s (Prensky 2003) and, therefore, are completely comfortable with (albeit sometimes overly-reliant on) the use of digital resources as part of their learning. These students are now described as 'digital natives', 'digital residents' and the 'net generation' – suggesting an innate confidence in using new technologies such as the internet, videogames, mobile telephony and 'all the other toys and tools of the digital age' (Prensky 2001, p.1). The implication within these discourses is that that these are students who know no other way than living with (and through) digital technology. Rather than using digital technology merely as part of their everyday lives, digital technology is seen as essential to these young people's existences – having grown up 'immersed' in these new technologies in ways that older generations were not (Prensky 2001). All told, many popular, political and academic commentators now presume a pressing need to re-arrange contemporary forms of education around students' affinity with digital technology and media.

As such, universities are now engaging in all manner of desperate attempts to meet the perceived digital needs and demands of a generation of students who are assumed to be yearning to connect, communicate and interact through digital technologies. Many universities and academic departments now have Facebook pages where students can become 'friends' with their institutions and tutors. Similar clumsy attempts to connect with students on their own digital terms can be seen in university uses of popular social media applications such as Twitter, Pinterest, Tumblr and Instagram. In a more tangible sense, many university campuses now offer free wireless internet connectivity, some universities have experimented with giving students subsidized tablet or laptop computers when enrolling, or paying for each student to have their own lifelong personal internet domain name. Universities are certainly putting a great deal of effort to 'catch-up' with the digital lifestyles of their students.

Of course, presumptions of a digital native generation of university students grossly over-simplify what is a far more complicated situation. The crude notion of there somehow being fundamental generational differences in attitudes and abilities to engage with digital technology has been roundly debunked and dismissed by critical commentators (see Buckingham 2011). Instead, it is beginning to be realized that there is a need to better understand the realities of students' use of digital technologies while at university, especially in terms of educationally-related engagement with digital technology. Similarly, more probing questions are beginning to be asked with regards to the role that digital technology is playing in the wider 'student experience' of twenty-first century university education. Growing numbers of critical commentators are therefore beginning to question the extent to which students are actually demanding to 'do' their studies via digital technologies and digital media.

Indeed, a small but growing body of research is beginning to paint a more nuanced picture of how students actually make use of digital technology during their university courses. This research has reported, for example, that students' academic use of the internet is heavily entwined with leisure uses, and tends to be curtailed by issues of time and motivation, as well as relevance to specific curricular and course assessment requirements (Gourlay 2014). While computer and smartphone use are major elements of students' working days, most research finds differences in terms of students' subject discipline and level of study, and often age, race and/or gender. Aside from these differences in engagement, there is mounting evidence that many students' *actual* uses of digital technologies remain rather more limited in scope than the digital native rhetoric would suggest. Studies of university students' technology use, for example, show a predominance of maintaining social network profiles, game playing, messaging and retrieval of online content (Madden et al. 2013, Paretta and Catalano 2013, Tindell and Bohlander 2012). Thus while some commentators may like to imagine collaborative communities of content creators, in reality many students' engagement with technology is often far more passive, solitary, sporadic and unspectacular, be it on or off campus (Livingstone 2009).

If anything, then, students' use of digital technologies – from undergraduate to postgraduate levels – can be described most accurately as involving the passive consumption of knowledge rather than the active creation of content – leading, at best, to what Crook (2008) terms a 'low bandwidth exchange' of information and knowledge, with any illusion of collaboration described more accurately in terms of cooperation or coordination between individuals. Students – both at undergraduate and postgraduate levels – have been found to be surprisingly ineffective in their use of the internet and other research tools. Indeed, Ian Rowlands and colleagues' (2008) study of 'The Google generation: the information behavior of the researcher of the future' highlighted a range of limitations to many university students' uses of online information. These included a tendency to skim documents, 'power browse' the abstracts of longer articles, or else 'squirrel away' digital content without reading it at all. In short, for many students digital information resources remain rather less expansive and empowering than the rhetoric of the digital native would lead us to believe.

Indeed, upon closer inspection much of this research conveys the sense that not *all* students are as inclined to integrate digital technologies into their studies as might be assumed. As is usually the case in educational debates, the suggested reasons for these disparities and divisions vary. Blame for these 'digital divisions' has been most frequently attributed to deficits of skills, motivation and know-how on the part of students, faculty and/or the educational institutions themselves. For example, some researchers have reasoned that university students' (non)engagement with the internet is influenced by perceptions of usefulness, ease-of-use and other psychological attitudes towards both technology and learning (e.g. Cheung and Huang 2005, Hong et al. 2003, Joiner et al. 2006). Differences in the quality of internet access have also been identified as a likely divide among students, most notably in terms of differences between 'public' and 'private' locations of use and forms of connectivity (Hassania 2006). Similarly, differences in institutional and faculty support and resourcing have also been raised as potentially inhibiting or facilitating factors (Eynon 2005). Questions have also been raised over the restrictive nature of the assessment and curriculum expectations that continue to underpin many forms of higher education study. For example, Brotcorne's (2005) qualitative study of Belgian undergraduates found internet use to often clash with (rather than complement) students' progress through the rigid systems of assessment, grading and academic conventions that constituted their degree programmes. This led Brotcorne (2005, n.p.) to conclude that students' use or non-use of the internet for their studies was not always due to a disadvantage per se but 'more due to matters of "digital choice" rather than "digital divide"'.

Recent surveys have tended to also portray university students' engagements with digital technologies as varied and often contrary to the notion of the all-knowing digital native. For example, Kennedy et al. (2010) highlighted four distinct groups of student technology users in Australian higher education – what they termed 'power users' (a minority of students who 'appropriate a wide range of technologies and use them significantly more frequently'); alongside the larger groups of 'ordinary users' and 'irregular users'. Most significant was the fourth category of 'basic users' – comprising nearly 50 percent of students 'characterized by extremely infrequent use of new and emerging technologies and less than weekly or monthly'. These types of use were found to vary considerably across different types of technology, and by different types of student – especially in terms of gender, university and cultural background. Similar conclusions regarding the highly varied use of digital technology and digital media emerged from Jones' (2012) 'net generation' study of UK universities. Here students were found to report varying levels of digital confidence and skills – often reporting 'initial surprise or confusion at the array of technologies that were available' (n.p.) and often willing to conform their technology use according to institutional requirements, university recommendations and course requirements. As the researchers concluded, 'the students distinguished between their actions as students and the actions they would take on their own behalf as private persons' – thus university-related technology use 'was not a direct expression of the self or personal values' (Jones and Healing 2010, p.352).

It is important, then, to approach students' uses of digital technology within higher education with a sense of caution and an acute awareness of context. There are clearly differences between how many students might be making use of digital technologies in their 'real lives' as opposed to the 'university lives'. In this sense, Gregor Kennedy et al. (2008, n.p.) make the useful distinction between 'living technologies' and 'learning technologies' – i.e. the difference between students 'everyday' skills with emerging technologies, as opposed to 'beneficial, technology based learning'. We therefore need to give further thought to the reasons why students are either engaging or not with specific forms of 'living' and 'learning' technologies – i.e. the roles that these technologies are playing in their lives, the meanings that are being attached to different digital practices and the outcomes and consequences of any use. In short, we need to develop a more socially sophisticated and sensitive understanding of the roles that digital technologies are playing the lives of university students and the various aspects of their 'work'. From this basis, student technology use can perhaps be best approached along three different lines of analysis – i.e. as a means of engaging with: (1) the academic requirements of university life; (2) the logistical requirements of university life; and (3) the social requirements of university life.

Digital technology and the academic requirements of student life

As was discussed in Chapter 3, such is the scope of the digital systems introduced into higher education over the past ten years or so that it is possible to successfully apply for, enroll in, complete and graduate from a university degree entirely through digital means. There are clearly many 'model' students who learn effectively and efficiently using the digital systems provided to them by their universities – combining these 'official' technologies with their own personal assemblages of devices, applications and tools (what educational technologists tend to refer to as 'personal learning networks'). Thriving communities of postgraduate research students on networks such as 'academia.edu' and 'ResearchGate' swapping references, tips, advice and engaging in meaningful discussions about their work. The vibrant Twitter stream of #phdchat is another element of how doctoral students engage with their work. Yet, as the surveys and studies just outlined suggest, these 'model' uses of digital learning are not reflected in how the majority of students appear to engage with their university studies. Instead, many students appear to be using digital technologies in less immersive, and perhaps more pragmatic, ways. Thus a sense emerges from the research literature of many students acting as 'savvy' but pressured consumers of higher education who engage with their studies – and therefore with 'learning technologies' – in considered and strategic ways. This strategic (non)engagement with technology can be seen in terms of a number of short-, medium- and longer-term issues that face most university students.

From a *short-term* perspective, the 'consequential validity' of assessment appears paramount to many students' engagement with digital technology – i.e. 'the effect of the test or other form of assessment on learning and other educational matters' (Boud 1995, p.38). For many university students, especially those studying subjects based around 'high-stakes' end-of-year examinations or final coursework assignments, the peripheral role that digital technology takes in the assessment demands of their university careers (besides the word-processing of essays and cursory searching of the internet for relevant information) provides a clear strategic impetus to rarely make extensive use of technology. Assessment is often viewed by students as a 'moral' activity by their tutors and universities, making it abundantly clear what is valued in the course and by higher education in general (Knight 1995). The fact that most university courses retain a focus on summative assessment and the 'culture of the grade' therefore shapes students' approaches to learning in limited 'syllabus-bound' ways (Norton et al. 2001). Thus the timed paper-and-pencil examination, the practical lab test and class-test all militate against extensive use of digital technologies – acting 'as a mechanism to control students that is far more pervasive and insidious than most staff would be prepared to acknowledge' (Boud 1995, p.38).

Similarly, the medium-term perspectives of many students on completing their university courses and being awarded a reasonable classification could be seen as not primarily 'digitally-dependent'. In the relatively short life of modular courses and ongoing coursework assessment there is often little time for students to develop new skills at the risk of jeopardizing the quality of their work and, ultimately, jeopardizing their final examination grades and grade classifications. Given the conflicting roles that digital technologies play in many university courses and programmes, students often have little medium-term incentive to continue to use technology and are compelled instead to adopt 'low-level' approaches to studying. As Sarah Mann (2001, p.7) observed of students entering UK universities:

> [M]any learners at different times tend to adopt either a surface approach to their study, characterized by a focus on rote learning, memorization and reproduction, a lack of reflection and a preoccupation with completing the task; or a strategic approach, characterized by a focus on assessment requirements and lecturer expectations, and a careful management of time and effort, with the aims of achieving high grades.

In this way, as with assessment, many students' apparent ambivalence towards digital technology could be seen as purely 'strategic' in the face of the growing external pressures to achieve satisfactory degree classifications (MacFarlane 1998). Such behaviour is certainly not a new phenomenon. Over forty years ago, Snyder (1971) demonstrated how college students quickly orientated themselves towards the 'hidden' rather than the formal curriculum and tailored their activities to what was tacitly expected of them. Given the purely incidental and conflicting role that digital technology continues to play in many degree courses, students have little medium-term incentive to continue to indulge in more expansive or niche digital practices that ultimately have little bearing on their eventual 'success'.

Even in terms of many students' longer-term perspective of gaining employment or continuing into further forms of university study, digital technology could be said to play a peripheral role. As their educational careers progress, students are encouraged to become 'portfolio people' (Wright et al. 1999), driven to build résumés, personal development plans and the like. Students are, of course, clear of the necessity to have a degree of competence with digital technology in order to gain employment but, nonetheless, are also clear in where 'IT skills' lays in relation to other desirable skills and competencies. Thus 'IT' is seen as being a basic, but not ultimately essential, element of developing one's 'marketability' to graduate employers. After fifteen years in technology-saturated school environments, many students are confident in their abilities to fulfil the levels of technology-related skills expected by future employers as and when required. Crucially, this ability to 'use IT' is often not seen as being contingent on sustained development of digital technology during their years of university study. This indifferent view of the ultimate currency of 'IT' mirrors a growing body of research into graduate employer demand for skills, which portrays a graduate labour market where overarching personal skills and qualities are valued far more highly by employers than any specific ability with digital technology or digital media.

Thus, rather than reflecting 'techno-phobic' or short-sighted attitudes and misconceptions, students' (non)use of digital technology during their academic studies could be seen a highly rational, empowered and pragmatic student body facing up to both the short- and long-term requirements posited by their university 'work' and future employment prospects. In choosing not to engage with some of the most educationally relevant or enhancing digital technologies on a regular or sustained basis, students may be prioritizing the use of digital technology against a host of other considerations and then acting accordingly. The fact that much use of digital technology (above and beyond word-processing, internet searching and access content from learning management systems) is neither advantageous nor required for the bulk of university study leaves many students in little doubt over its place. It would seem that for many students *not* making particularly expansive use of digital technology is simply a pragmatic response to the short-term demands of their studies and then gaining employment, rather than a deep-rooted technological inability or long-term ignorance.

Digital technology and the logistical requirements of student life

As these latter issues suggest, it is important not to see students' engagement with digital higher education solely in terms of 'learning'. Much of how and why students make use of digital technology is less related to the act of learning, and more to the rather more pragmatic issues of 'doing education'. The lived experience of digital higher education is rather less rarefied and academically focused than educationalists and educators would like to imagine. These issues have been foregrounded in studies of how university students make use of social networks such as Facebook – teasing out the place of their university studies amidst the social milieu of social networking. These studies rarely report instances of Facebook being used to sustain student 'learning' per se. However, students' networks of social media and communications technologies are found to be an important means of how students 'do university' – in other words, how they negotiate the logistical demands of their work as students. This logistical 'work' also involves attending lectures, classes and tutorials – dealing with last-minute room changes and required preparatory work. This involves the production of assignments, essays and coursework – all of which have specific requirements for word-count, form and structure, timing of submission and so on. These logistical demands increase dramatically during examination and assessment periods – with students having to deal with an overload of information relating to when, where and in what forms they are required to be assessed. On top of all these learning-related logistics are a host of deadlines, requirements and demands relating to the financial and legal aspects of 'being' a university student.

Unsurprisingly, research finds university students to be making extensive use of digital technologies in dealing with these aspects of their work. A study of UK students, for example, highlighted the sporadic and often uncomfortable intrusion of university education into students' private digital lives (Selwyn 2009). The study illustrated the fluctuating prominence of educational concerns within students' overall use of Facebook, with instances of education-related interactions between students structured by the rhythms of assessment schedules or timetabled teaching provision rather than a desire for forms of continuous learning or *ad hoc* educational exchange. Much of these students' 'educational' use of Facebook was therefore based around the exchange of logistical or factual information about teaching and assessment requirements – drawing on networks of peers to swap information, understandings and tips about what they were supposed to be doing. Digital technologies such as Facebook therefore were seen as a ready means of 'working around' unreliable official sources of information, as well as compensating for students' non-engagement with official information (missing lectures, not reading emails and so on). In this sense, students were found to have developed extensive 'shadow networks' of university-related information and advice. Thus, while Facebook was not an important element of students' academically related learning, it was a useful means of engaging with university studies.

This use of digital technology as a means of 'getting by' when negotiating the demands of university study are also reflected in the rather more murky area of what is often described officially as 'academic malpractice'. Indeed, the copying, falsification and plagiarism of essays and assignments has long been a prevalent form of academic misconduct within undergraduate student populations. Yet the increasing ubiquity of internet use within higher education settings has heightened academic concerns over the prevalence of online plagiarism and 'cyber-cheating'. As Paulhus et al. (2003, p.2) described over ten years ago:

> [A]cademic cheating is now easier than ever. Instead of typing up another student's term paper, students can now simply copy their file. Instead of typing up text from an internet source, students can simply copy the information electronically. For a fee, one can access prepared papers from any one of 251 internet 'paper mills' (at last count). Papers on any topic, at any level of sophistication can be downloaded in a matter of seconds.

University authorities and teaching staff have been quick to recognize online plagiarism as a serious form of academic malpractice – devoting considerable efforts and resources towards the implementation of online plagiarism detection services and other computer-based strategies to counter such digital 'dishonesty'. This has resulted in what Young (2001) describes as a 'cat-and-mouse game of plagiarism detection' between university authorities and students, now constituting a multi-million dollar, time-consuming element of university administration.

While some of the recent fears surrounding internet plagiarism could be said to have approached something of a moral panic, it has been reckoned that substantial proportions of university students indulge in some form of plagiarism via online sources – from 'cutting and pasting' a few unattributed sentences or paragraphs into an assignment through to purchasing a ghost-written essay from internet-based 'paper mills'. One US study, for example, found over 50 per cent of university students to report involvement in some form of internet-based academic cheating during their university career (Breen and Maassen 2005). Analysis of business studies assignments submitted to one New Zealand institution found that around 25 per cent contained plagiarism, with one-tenth extensively plagiarized (Walker 2010). Similarly, studies in North American, UK and Australian higher education institutions have found between 30 and 40 per cent of undergraduate students admitting to 'importing' online material into their assignments without acknowledging the source, and between 10 per cent and 20 per cent admitting to doing so for substantial proportions of an assignment (Christensen and McCabe 2006, McGowan 2005). This figure is reckoned to be around one-quarter of graduate students (McCabe 2005).

While there is some consensus around the general prevalence of online plagiarism within student populations, there is less agreement as to the rationales, motivations and reasoning underpinning such behaviours. For some commentators, students' internet-based plagiarism is seen as being led directly by the structure and nature of the internet itself – not least the abundant access to information sources. In this sense online plagiarism can be seen as constituting a form of 'electronic opportunism' (Rocco and Warglien 1995). Reiterating this theme of internet-led behaviour, other researchers have portrayed online plagiarism as a facet of the altered sense of morality amongst younger generations when operating in online contexts. The suggestion has been made, for example, that students perceive online plagiarism offences as being significantly less dishonest than similar offences using printed sources (Gullifer and Tyson 2010, 2014).

The circumstances and motivations underpinning this facet of 'digital higher education' are clearly complicated, yet could be seen as a continuation of the less 'inappropriate' digital practices outlined before. Indeed, another group of commentators portray students' online plagiarism as less determined by the internet per se, but instead reflecting the changing nature of the student experience within the massified university systems of the early twenty-first century. Thus online plagiarism is argued to stem from the increased competitiveness and pressure felt by students to achieve high grades and a 'good' overall degree classification. Moreover, students are argued to be facing a host of more immediate issues such as time constraints to produce written work and alienation from legitimate sources of academic support due to the inaccessibility of teaching staff and library resources (Breen and Maassen 2005, Underwood and Szabo 2004, Ashworth et al. 1997). From this perspective, digital 'cheating' could be seen as a necessary survival technique for some students – less of an individual deficit, but more of a collectively acceptable means of 'getting by'.

Digital technology and the social requirements of student life

Whether using digital technology in an illicit or approved manner, so far we have considered students' use of digital technology primarily in terms of engagement with academic activities. The most prevalent aspects of students' digital practices, however, relate to what could be termed the social requirements of the 'work' of being a student – i.e. being a student in a social rather than academic sense. Personal uses of digital technology such as social networking, mobile telephony and so on are clearly an integral element of student life. The internet has certainly become enmeshed into 'daily lives and the social interactions' of educated, well-resourced, middle-class university students (McMillan and Morrison 2006, p.74). While perhaps ignored as part of their university studies, applications such as Facebook and Twitter provide most university students with an extensive social information and communications environment. What Kennedy terms 'living technologies' are therefore an integral element of the contemporary university student experience – what Ana Aleman and Katherine Wartman (2009) term 'online campus culture' (p.ix). With this thought in mind, we also need to examine how 'college and university students appreciate, value, construct, and negotiate student culture online' (p.ix).

One important role that digital technology plays in this sense is as a means of students' development and maintenance of social capital. For some well-resourced and well-motivated students, digital technologies are clearly a ready means of developing and sustaining contacts and connections required for future study and employment. Russell Francis' (2010) study of doctoral students at Oxford

University showed, for example, how networks such as LinkedIn were used to develop high-level contacts with strategically important individuals, and how these connections were later used to secure employment. Of course, doctoral students at Oxford are a rather privileged example, endowed with many different forms of offline social connections and advantage. More common is students' use of digital technology to maintain and sustain social networks – both with the university peer-groups, and with friends from previous stages of their lives (such as school friends), family members and other acquaintances. As a study of UK undergraduate students by Madge et al. (2009) reported, Facebook was an important social tool used by the majority of the respondents to aid the 'settling in' process at university – especially in terms of acting as part of the 'social glue' that aided newly enrolled students as they adjusted to university life. Digital applications such as Facebook were an integral element of being connected into campus social events – receiving invitations, registering one's interest and generally maintaining involvement in social activities

While such uses of digital technology are perhaps to be expected, one of the more interesting themes to emerge from studies of these aspects of student technology use is the tendency for online social networks to reinforce – rather than disrupt – differences in social contact. This is most noticeable in terms of race, class and gender. Broadly, it is reported that white, middle class, male students are most likely to maintain online networks of similar friends and acquaintances. Conversely, black students appear to also seek out similarity along the same lines. Thus, as Mayer and Puller's (2008) study of social network formation on US college campuses reported, the strongest predictor of whether two students are 'friends' on Facebook was race – even after controlling for a variety of measures of socioeconomic background, ability, and college activities. As such, it would appear that digital technologies are used primarily for maintaining strong links between people already in relatively tight-knit, emotionally close offline relationships, rather than creating new points of contact with a 'glocalized' community of students from other courses or even institutions (McMillan and Morrison 2006). In this sense it could be concluded that digital technologies such as Facebook perpetuate an 'offline to online trend' in that they sustain geographically-bound campus communities, as opposed to the 'online to offline trend' where people meet up with previously unknown online 'buddies' in real life (Ellison et al. 2007).

Aside from using digital technology to develop social connections, another significant element of student life reflected in digital technology use is simply for communication, gossip and what can be termed 'banter'. As Selwyn's (2009) study reported, much of students' 'educational' use of Facebook actually concerned either the post-hoc critiquing of learning experiences and events; instances of supplication and moral support with regards to assessment or learning; and the promotion of oneself as academically incompetent and/or disengaged. In this sense, Facebook postings were merely continuations of the informal discourses that have long characterized student life. Selwyn contended that the online exchanges found in this research were merely a continuation of how students talk to each other in other contexts – such as the chatter of the back rows of the lecture theatre, coffee shop or after-college telephone conversations. The key difference with Facebook was, as Kirkpatrick (2005, p.156) acknowledges, that the 'playful banter and chit-chat which are always present in the murmuring noise that we are aware of in a class are sanitized and included as on an equal level with the "official" discourse of the classroom'.

In this sense, digital technologies such as Facebook can be seen as important sites for the informal, cultural learning of 'being' a student, with online interactions and experiences allowing roles to be learnt, values understood and identities shaped. Studies such as Selwyn's show students coming to terms with the roles and the nuances of the 'undergrad' culture within which they found themselves located. Students' Facebook use both reflected and was part of the 'intricate hierarchies, rich organizational traditions and interpersonal ties' of higher education (Hewitt and Forte 2006, p.1) – not least the existing social relations and practices of the 'real communities' of their university, department and classes. Facebook should therefore be seen as an increasingly important element of students' meaning-making activities, especially where they reconstruct past events and thereby confer meaning onto the overarching university experience.

Digital technology therefore needs to be recognized as an important element of students' identity formation and impression management – especially the notion that students' use of social media is governed by the degree to which they felt able to control and regulate their online presentation of self. In this sense Selwyn's (2009) study of student Facebook use reflected many of the themes from the general literature on the university student experience – i.e. a distancing and alienation from remote and aloof teachers (Haggis 2006), unease at 'the power relations that surround students as they are assessed' (Barrow 2006, p.357), the impact of term-time working on the student experience (Little 2002), the fragmented commitment to an intellectual 'vocation' (Dubet 2004) and a lack of experience and/or interest in learning an academic subject. In all these instances, students' social uses of digital technology can be seen to reflect the hurried, distantiated and disjointed realities of undergraduate education. Thus it could be concluded that Facebook *is* an important education-related technology of twenty-first century higher education – albeit one that contributes to what Kitto and Higgins (2003, p.49) term 'the production of the university as an ambivalent space'.

Indeed, it could be argued that social media applications such as Facebook act as ideal sites for what Erving Goffman (1961) termed 'role distance' – situations where students can distance themselves from roles which have to be enacted but with which they do not necessarily wish to be identified by others. For example, Selwyn's study found some students seeking to maintain a degree of personal autonomy by engaging in the minimum of overly academic behaviour expected of being an undergraduate scholar and/or were acting in ways that exhibited their lack of commitment to the role. On Facebook students could rehearse and explore resistance to the academic 'role set' of being an undergraduate (Merton 1957) – i.e. the expected and 'appropriate' behaviours towards their subject disciplines, teachers and university authorities. Students who were facing conflicting demands in their roles as socialites, minimum-wage earners and scholars could use Facebook as an arena for developing disruptive, challenging, dismissive and/or unruly academic identities. Thus Facebook was acting as a ready space for resistance and the contestation of the asymmetrical power relationship built into the established offline positions of university, student and lecturer (Bourdieu and Passeron 1977). This was perhaps most clearly evident in the playful and often ironic rejection of dominant university discourses throughout students' online interactions, with the students certainly not confirming to the passive and silenced undergraduate roles of the seminar room or lecture theatre.

Of course, these uses of digital technology to support and extend student culture may not reflect wholly desirable aspects of student life. This is apparent, for example, in the recent fad for UK students to create university-specific 'Spotted' pages on Facebook where anonymous descriptions and comments on other students seen around the campus can be posted and commented on. On the one hand, these pages can be seen as harmless 'banter'; on the other hand they can be seen as a form of predatory peer surveillance and verbal bullying. As Jaffer (2013, n.p.) describes, these sites are 'meant to provide comic relief for procrastinating students. Inevitably, though, they have become a hotbed of sneering jibes and vicious gossip.' Similarly controversial but popular websites such as 'Uni-Lad' in the UK, offer spaces for students to engage in what many people would consider to be inappropriate misogynist, racist and sexist behaviour that would be much less acceptable in offline campus spaces.

Making sense of students and digital technology

Digital technology use is clearly entwined with the complex 'work' of being a university student. As such, the fact that students' use of digital technology for direct engagement with academic work or learning is sporadic and inconsistent is perhaps not surprising. University students should clearly not be seen as cohorts of 'digital natives' whose *entire* lives are mediated through digital technologies. On one hand, then, it is important to recognize that much of the academic and learning requirements of university study can be negotiated quite effectively with a limited engagement with digital technologies. At best, for many students, digital technology could be said to reflect distinct forms of 'defensive learning' – reflecting the ambivalent, contradictory and often half-hearted efforts of university authorities and teaching staff to develop digital provision. As Standing (2011, p.72) observes, contemporary forms of university education could be seen as a variation on the 'old Soviet joke in which the workers said, "They pretend to pay us, we pretend to work." The education variant would be as follows: "They pretend to educate us, we pretend to learn."' On the other hand, it is important to recognize the fact that the 'life world' of being a 'student' within the massified higher education landscape often has little to do with issues of intellectual endeavour or collaborative learning per se but is predicated upon successful negotiation of the logistical demands of part-time paid employment, university coursework and exams, as well as the attendant coping strategies of socializing and the 'downtime' associated with the student lifestyle.

Indeed, all of the issues discussed above suggest that students' uses and non-uses of digital technologies should be seen as 'a form of good sense' in terms of their wider understandings about their work (Gitlin and Margonis 1995). It is important to note here how students' readings might differ considerably from those of their teachers or university authorities. As Bauman (2005, p.28) argues, 'the meaning of education' is an obvious instance where 'the perceptions of the "teaching" and the "taught" classes diverge. And no wonder, given the difference between the frames within which their respective lives are woven, as well as between the respective life experiences on which they reflect.'

The same thesis can therefore be applied to students' engagements with digital technologies – acknowledging the fact that students face a markedly different set of priorities, pressures and preoccupations than their teachers. As Masterman and Shuyska (2012, p.349) concluded from their study of master's students and digital technology:

> One cannot ignore the interplay between the digital and the non-digital technologies that runs as a leitmotif through students' experiences . . . On occasion, students will make conscious choices not to engage with digital technologies. This does not necessarily mark them out as 'Luddite'; rather, it can be indicative of self-knowledge (what is right for them) or, even, an awareness that more fundamental principles may come into play in their choices.

In this sense, students' uses of digital technologies can be seen in terms of a pragmatic negotiation of work – i.e. meaning-making and fitting digital technology with their own 'lived' experiences of being a student. This perspective necessitates an understanding of the act of what is required of 'being a student' in social, economic, political as well as educational terms. As studies of contemporary young adulthood show, it is clear that there is a lot more to the 'job' of being a student than learning with (or without) digital technology – not least the juggling of a number of academic and non-academic demands during a university career that places students in various conflicting roles such as learner, peer, son/daughter, socialite, part-time employee and prospective employee. All of these spheres of students' life worlds should therefore be seen as having a bearing on their use of digital technology in university.

Of course, it would be unwise to construct a wholly agentic account of students' experiences of their engagements with digital technology. Consideration should also be given to the ways in which issues such as social class, race, gender and disability mediate students' educational experiences with technology. There is clear evidence from the existing empirical literature of the various ways in which nature and outcomes of digital technology use differs within student populations in terms of age, social class, race and gender. Indeed, studies have detailed the comparatively expansive ways that digital technologies tend to be deployed with students from relatively privileged backgrounds. Overall, a consistent picture emerges of how digital technology appears to contribute to – rather than overcome – differences between and within student populations, with inequalities of gender, race and class reproduced through digital technology. As such, students' digital technology use would appear to be something that is more often entwined with (rather than disruptive of) the subtle but well-established internal processes of stratification within university populations. For instance, the reproductive function of digital technology can also be seen in terms of the processes of students' identity formation described earlier. Digital technology use has long been found to offer a ready space where the 'role conflicts' that students often experience in their relationships with their peers, teaching staff, academic work and so on are worked out. An important point that should not be overlooked, however, is the extent to which these unofficial uses subvert students' gendered identities, social positions and relations. The casual sexism, homophobia and misogyny on 'Uni-Lad' and 'Spotted' webpages may well be amplifying the divisive bullying and misogynist nature of offline campus culture, rather than challenging it.

Moreover, these stratifications could well have a social class dimension. Of concern here is the extent to which digital technologies are implicit in the perpetuation of a second-rate university education in preparation for second-rate forms of graduate employment. It could be argued that the short-termist, fragmented, multi-tasking, disengaged and alienated ways in which many university students are engaging with digital higher education is developing and reinforcing many of the dispositions and qualities required for the low-status information processing jobs that they are set to take up after their studies. These are forms of technology use that are compatible with what Standing (2011) identifies as 'precarious' labour – i.e. the flexible, unstable and instrumental jobs of the information age, based around a floating but rudderless direction, characterized by increased anomie, anxiety and alienation. After exiting the formal education system with a college or a university degree, all but the most privileged and fortunate of students will experience a decidedly precarious existence throughout their twenties. This is certainly reinforced by their engagements with digital technology, which could be seen as functioning subtly to 'stream youth into the flexible labour system, based on a privileged elite, a small technical working class and a growing precariat' (Standing 2011, p.72).

Conclusions

This chapter has developed an argument that various aspects of the 'work' of being a university student influence the use of digital technology. Clearly, students' uses of digital technologies during their university studies tend to be numerous but disparate and often ad hoc. As Gourlay and Oliver (2013, p.93) conclude, students' technology use is perhaps best understood as 'characterized by multiple spaces and domains of engagement, the centrality of networked devices, and the highly contingent, negotiated nature of practices which [a]re adapted and co-constituted through small, everyday engagements with technologies'.

In particular, when making sense of the quotidian characteristics of technology use, we need to remain mindful of the 'fit' between digital technology and three aspects of student life – (1) engaging with academic demands of university studies; (2) managing the logistical aspects of study; and (3) negotiating the social requirements of student life. On one hand, it is clear how digital technologies now play a key part in the social and logistical elements of the university 'student experience'. On the other hand, digital technology also appears to have a more compromised relationship with academic learning – with students often able to make instrumental use of institutionally 'approved' technologies in order to fulfil the requirements of their academic courses. Crucially, this distinction between 'living' and 'learning' technologies may well exacerbate entrenched patterns and processes of stratification within student populations.

So, a lot of ground has been covered in the first five chapters of this book. Digital technology use in higher education clearly is shaped by the many different structures and systems that exist within universities, and the many different people who 'work' in some form within higher education. Digital higher education clearly is a socio-technical affair. But what about the *physical* realities of higher education in the digital age? Having considered the digital systems, digital work, digital study and digital life that all are part of digital higher education, it is now time to consider a rather less obvious aspect – the materialities of digital technology use in higher education. How are digital technologies written into the objects, artefacts, places, physical appearances and spatial arrangements of universities?

Chapter 6

Digital 'stuff'

Digital technology and the materialities of the university

Introduction

As well as being comprised of organizational systems, people and their work, universities are also tangible places and tangible 'things'. The most obvious tangible elements are the buildings in which universities are based and the wider campus spaces that they fill – the plazas and the quads, the tower blocks, redbrick facades and glass-plate frontages, and other nooks and crannies. Within these buildings are the office spaces of academics, lecture theatres, seminar rooms and study spaces. Alongside these are libraries, students' unions, shops, refectories, coffee shops and so on. All of these spaces provide a material context for digital higher education. Crucially, these material features are key elements in the production, consumption and ordering of the 'university'. In contrast to our previous discussions, this chapter considers the materialities of universities in the digital age – the physical environments, the material objects within them, and the spatial arrangements that continue to constitute the university as a 'place'. In so doing, we will focus on a number of deceptively simple questions:

- How is the material culture of the digital university performed?
- To what extent do the spaces and material objects of the university constitute a framework for situated digital action – shaping the ways that digital technologies are (not) used?
- To what extent are digital practices and processes resulting in new spaces, objects and material arrangements?

In short, this chapter considers the bearing of the material relations of the university on digital higher education. In so doing, it first helps to consider briefly what these different concepts mean. First and foremost, this chapter relates to what is known in some parts of the social sciences as 'material culture' i.e. the study of the tangible objects, 'things' and 'stuff' of everyday life that are constructed by humans. The academic study of material culture is notably exhaustive in its coverage, concerning itself with anything from a single button on a coat to a whole city (Ferguson 1977). As such, the value of considering the material culture of any particular segment of society is what it can tell us about the wider social relations and social arrangements of that segment of society. As Schlereth (1982, p.3) reasons, through material culture we can learn about the 'belief systems – the values, ideas, attitudes, and assumptions – of a particular community or society, usually across time'.

Of particular significance to this book are the material characteristics of the built university environment. In this sense, the notion of the university as 'place' is of particular relevance i.e. the bringing together of things and spaces within given boundaries, with imputed values and interpretations (O'Toole and Were 2008). Thus we are not interested solely in university buildings, but in the places that university buildings form. Of course, places are best understood as being socially constructed – as Gaffin (1996, p.76) puts it, 'people make spaces into places'. Thus, we need to remain mindful that while a place such as a university library building is (almost) always constructed with definite purposes in mind, they are usually then re-interpreted and re-determined by subsequent occupiers (or users) of that place. Making sense of what places were designed to be, and what they later become is therefore an important element of understanding any social practice. This is certainly the case in terms of higher education. The difference between teaching in a drafty, dilapidated lecture theatre and a bespoke learning hub are obvious. Thus, it is important to consider the shaping influence of places on social action and social practices. Indeed, research studies suggest that what students learn is greatly influenced by the designed features of the 'holistic' classroom environment, such as layout, lighting, noise and even colour (Barrett et al. 2013). The key questions for this particular chapter, therefore, are to what extent do such decidedly non-digital aspects of the university shape digital technology use? Conversely, how is the material substance of the university altering to accommodate digital technology?

Rebuilding the university for the digital age – from new 'builds' to old 'work-arounds'

Universities have long sought to define themselves through their architecture – from the dreaming spires of Oxford through to the brand new campuses and satellite sites of more recent institutions. The past forty years have seen universities of varying size and status around the world indulge in increasingly ostentatious 'statement' architecture. Often these public displays of innovation and modernity have been most pronounced in lesser, 'up-and-coming' institutions that could perhaps be seen to have 'something to prove'. In London, for example, the lowly ranked London Metropolitan University issued a bold statement of intent at the end of the 1990s by commissioning a £3 million Graduate Centre building designed by Daniel Libeskind – a high-profile 'starchitect' of the time. While the resulting metal-clad angular building garnered fulsome praise from the architecture establishment it also provoked bewilderment (bordering on anger) from many local residents. Whatever your reaction, the Graduate Centre is certainly now an incongruous feature of North London's grimy Holloway Road. At the same time and on the opposite side of the world, the Royal Melbourne

Institute of Technology (RMIT) (another institution that would not usually be classed a top-tier university) is well into a long-term programme of audacious building and renovation projects, which has seen all manner of bulbous, jagged and asymmetrical buildings added to Melbourne's city-centre urban environment.

Many of these buildings provide very public reflections of the digital age university. The design of RMIT's Swanston Academic building, for example, was justified as a building to support interactivity and connectivity – full of 'portal spaces' for enabling technology use (Crafti 2012). In the UK, Salford University's £50 million 'Digital Campus' space within the city's 'Media City' complex espoused similar aims – in the words of its inaugural director: 'This is a digital futures campus. It is not a place you come to read books. It is a place to do real work on real-time digital platforms. You are not messing around – you are in the real world' (Jon Corner, cited in Brown 2011, n.p.).

These are by no means peculiarly British or Australian trends. Take, for instance, Cornell University's $2 billion mid-river 'Silicon Island' project on Roosevelt Island, or Malaysia's establishment of a 'Multimedia University' within an entire internet-focused city (the CyberJaya project). As projects such as these suggest, higher education institutions around the world have spent the past few decades literally remoulding themselves in the image of the digital age – with varying degrees of success and elegance.

However, these flagship examples notwithstanding, the material reconstruction of university campuses is often smaller-scale, more prosaic and more ad hoc in nature. These high-profile renewal and renovation projects obscure the fact that most university activity is housed within existing architectural forms that are rather less deliberately planned and designed. Instead, the usual built environment of the university is notoriously messy and haphazard. Thus from the sixteenth-century cloisters of Oxford and Cambridge to the pre-fabricated 1960s' facades of less prestigious institutions, digital technology has been fitted clumsily around the decaying built environments of universities that can ill-afford to maintain the buildings that they already have, let alone make further additions.

The diversity of contemporary university built environments fits with the distinction made by Nansen et al. (2011) with regards to the varying gradations of domestic architecture. These authors suggest that at one extreme is what can be termed the '*designed*' home – i.e. where families imagine what is necessary for their dwelling and then design a house accordingly – replete with bespoke structure, skin, space-plan, services and other 'stuff'. Of course, most people are not in the privileged position of being able to 'start from scratch' in this way. Some people will opt for the '*renovated*' home – where the existing structure, design and arrangements of a dwelling are reconstructed in a reflexive response to new needs. Of course, most people can neither afford nor have the time for either of these options. A more pragmatic third response, therefore, is to live in the '*found*' home, where inhabitants are forced to adjust their belongings, spatial arrangements and practices to accommodate to the existing structure, layout and arrangement of the house.

Of course, these varying arrangements have varying influences on the use of technology and media – whether in a family home or a university campus. Indeed, this continuum from 'bespoke' to 'found' has been well noted by anthropologists, cultural geographers and architectural historians, who have all detailed how the 'stuff' of new technology interplays with the material culture of institutional settings such as the home. For instance, Rybczynski's (1986) historical analysis of the changing shape of households over the twentieth century illustrated how the industrial technologies of gas, electricity and telephones presented a challenge to the structure of houses by demanding their own space, and almost inevitably affecting the development of the layout and use of domestic settings over time. Similarly, Lynn Spigel's (1992) 'media archaeology' research has detailed how the material and social structure of homes in North America were redesigned to 'make room' for television. This was the case for the physical device of the television 'set' and its associated wiring, but also the shifting practices, social ideals and widening spatial horizons of 1950s' post-war living associated with the medium of television. Spigel describes the 'dialogical relationship' between television and the material culture of the home, with some families in the 1950s placing televisions in decorative settings, making a 'feature' of them, accompanied by furniture ensembles, lighting and even wallpaper 'entirely organized around the television set' (Spigel 1992, p.107).

If we approach the materialities of the university and digital technology in a similar manner to that of the domestic house, then contemporary universities see some people operating within newly designed places while others are squeezed in and around long-existing arrangements. On one hand, as Rachel Hurdley (2010) observes, many universities are embracing the new architecture of the open-plan office, indoor street, forum and atrium – all designed in a spirit of 'openness' and 'connectivity' associated with digital higher education. Yet clearly for every newly imagined and designed 'digital campus' there are a hundred 'found' counterparts where digital technologies are squeezed, bent and forced around what went before. These found arrangements constitute the entwining of architectures from previous centuries with the practices of the early twenty-first century – with understandably varying degrees of comfort, elegance and practicality. Clearly, then, we need to pay closer attention to how these different forms of built environment interact with digital media use, and what forms of mutually shaping relationships exist between these material contexts and digital practices, processes and forms. It is therefore worth taking a little time to consider the range of built environments that the contemporary digital university finds itself materially situated within.

Mapping out the spaces and places of the digital university

University libraries

Perhaps the most interesting place to begin examining the materialities of digital higher education is part of the university that is traditionally seen as most threatened by digitization. As such, university libraries have been often particularly prominent beneficiaries (or, if you prefer, victims) of digitally driven designs, renovations and work-arounds. Libraries – as resource repositories, places for learning and spaces to socialize are therefore ideal examples of the spaces and places of the contemporary digital university.

Over the past ten years or so, universities have tended to not build new 'libraries' per se. Instead, we have seen the commissioning and construction of multi-million dollar 'learning hubs', 'learning resource centres' and the like. These newly imagined and designed facilities still make room for collections of books, but also house all manner of spaces to support digital devices and digital practices. The main library in Helsinki University – opened in 2012 – is one such example. The architectural brief for this building reflected the subtle influences that digital technologies are having on contemporary university librarianship. For example, at the time of the new design the university's libraries were reckoned to be using 70 per cent of their acquisition funds on digital – rather than printed – resources. The university authorities also reckoned that science and medicine users almost exclusively preferred to access and use digital resources, with only humanities students and researchers having a sustained need for physical books. The building brief therefore placed an emphasis on the building acting as a space for people to come and use their own devices, to interact with each other and also to relax and rest. As the architects put it: 'to sum up, the keywords are diversity, flexibility, convertibility and support for interaction' (Sinikara 2013, p.8).

The resulting building is housed in a large glass-fronted building, swathed in natural light, curved internal balconies and sweeping arcs. Alongside shelving for its 1.5 million-volume collection, the library boasts open-plan spaces for studying and relaxation, closed-off spaces for discussion and group study, alongside a number of 'break' rooms and café spaces. The building's 'fluidity' is reflected in a range of furniture – from 'La-Z-Boy'-style reclining chairs, study pods and rows of more utilitarian workbenches with electricity sockets and wireless connectivity. As might be expected, digital technology plays a key role in the functioning of this library. Users are expected to use their own portable devices, and are provided with a range of automated library services based around the attachment of radio-frequency identification (RFID) tags to all physical resources. Self-service issuing machines allow users to check out and check in materials themselves, rather than using a librarian. Robotized 'returns sorters' have been installed to aid the re-shelving process, automated units for the payment of fines, and even 'intelligent trolleys' that monitor which materials have been used but not removed from the library.

While the University of Helsinki has devoted considerable resources to this design, far more universities have opted to refurbish and renovate the library buildings that they already have along less extensive lines. The move towards 'library 2.0' has – of course – seen the insertion of extensive computing and printing facilities, primarily to support students' on-campus studies. These are variously housed in vast computer-lab style rooms with rows of desk-bound machines, more loosely designed spaces where students can connect devices wirelessly while sat on couches, benches and cubby-holes. Much of the same technology found in the Helsinki 'new build' are also in evidence, although often less elegantly proportioned and arranged given the confines of buildings designed primarily for book collections, librarian-run issue desks and studying with paper documents. The £20 million refurbishment of the University of York's main 'JB Morrell Library' is one such example. The refurbished building is now free of asbestos, and has new heating, lighting and ventilation systems, alongside remodelled walls and ceilings. The main result of this reshaping has been the provision of what the university describes as 'IT-rich study and research areas'. Thus, in the university's words, 'all areas are IT enabled' either with desktop computers or the requisite power sockets and wireless internet connectivity for portable computing devices. Spatially, computers are clustered in either 'quiet' or 'silent' zones, alongside areas for 'open collaborative' work, and intriguingly named 'research hotels' (actually temporary offices for visiting researchers and academics).

Of course, many libraries have received considerably less attention and resources, left instead to cope with the influx of digitized resources and technology-using students as best they can. Often these libraries now come across as cramped, chaotically arranged amalgams of a 1960s library and an office from the mid-2000s when desktop computing and photocopying remained prominent technologies. Computer terminals dedicated to searching library catalogues and managing individual accounts have long been dotted around university libraries. The borrowing of books and journals takes place through the means of barcode readers, swipe cards and self-issue and self-return vending machines. Computers for student use are crammed into small rooms, or to the side of bookshelves and study desks. All in all, the stilted atmosphere (and stilted working arrangements) of the traditional university library remains – albeit with an over-layer of digital technologies. Cabling is usually 'trunked' onto the outside of walls. Traces of previous technologies remain – from microfiche readers and card indexes, to understaffed issue and enquiry desks. One of the consequences of the insertion of more technology is often a perceptible loss of space. Some libraries have been forced to make room by reducing the gaps between stacks of books to the bare minimum, often requiring any library visitor to walk through sideways. Other libraries have systems of vault-like, high-density 'mobile shelving systems' where shelves have to be pulled out individually by the library users as required. The resulting environment often conveys a sense of partially digitized scholarship with much of the life sucked out of it.

Lecture theatres and other teaching spaces

Another aspect of the university built environment shaped by the use of digital technologies are the teaching spaces – the lecture theatres, seminar rooms, workshops and the like. There are architectural forms that have been influenced by decades (if not centuries) of pedagogical assumptions and institutional priorities. Digital technologies are therefore shaped by the grammar and rubric of these spaces, as well as having a bearing on the development over time. For example, regardless of pedagogic diversity, the design of newly built lecture theatres remains predicated upon the practice of projecting information to a large group of students sitting in front of – or around – a lecturer. The centrality of the projection of digital images onto screens dictates the length, width and breath of these spaces. Architectural guidelines for screen viewing suggest that distances between audience and image should be between two and six times the width of the screen. Room width is governed by viewing angle (under UK guidelines, for example, this should be a maximum of 40 degrees), speech projection angles (90 degrees maximum). Newly designed lecture theatres often achieve this in a highly stylized manner. While rammed full of laptops, internet access, data projectors, audio systems, large multiple projection screens and multi-dimensional sound systems, they retain a calm sense of immersion. These are spaces intended not to distract from the content of the lecture. The need to see the projected images usually negates the use of natural light, but complex systems of dimmable 'mood' lighting are designed to ensure visibility of individual's work and more distant projections. Raked rows of seats offer optimal sightlines, with pivoting tables for writing and typing, electricity sockets and wireless connectivity. Internal acoustic quality is coupled with the need to usually isolate the lecture theatre from external events through soundproofing and double-glazing.

Similar issues shape the design of other teaching spaces, such as seminar rooms, design workshops and laboratories. Perhaps the most 'digitally shaped' teaching spaces currently to be found in some universities are the latest incarnations of the 'cave automatic virtual environment' (usually referred to by the self-referencing acronym CAVE). These are rooms with LED display (walls, and sometimes ceilings and floors) allowing the immersive projection of 2D and 3D environments. The experience of these rooms is akin to being wrapped in a cinema screen, and can allow classes to be immersed in a simulated environments (from a patient's arteries to the surface of Mars) or to explore data representations in 3D. Some universities have less sophisticated 'green screen' rooms, allowing similar forms of immersive projection. Science and medicine departments may have computer-based simulation rooms – where laboratories or surgical theatres can be simulated for training purposes. All in all, a variety of bespoke high-tech teaching and learning spaces can be found throughout university campuses.

Of course, university teaching and learning usually takes place in settings that are a lot more unplanned and organic than this. The majority of lecture theatres, seminar rooms and tutorial spaces were not designed specifically for digital technology use, and have been subjected to regular fitting and refitting of various generations of teaching and learning technologies. The typical teaching space of the 2010s may well have data projectors hanging from ceilings or fixed into boxes towards the back of the room. These are usually in fixed positions that dictate the use of the room in ways that direct people towards the gaze of the projected image. There may well be a lectern with a computer secreted inside – sometimes accessible to the lecturer, sometimes not. These may be a separate sound system that often allows for the audio recording of the session as well as the in-class play-back of sound. There may be a lighting system with adjustable settings depending on the nature of the technology being used – projected images usually requiring the dimming of lights. Often, there might be remnants of previous eras of edu-cational technology relegated to the sides and corners of the room – electronic whiteboards still fixed to walls, televisions and video recorders, light bulb driven overhead projectors, and odd assortments of sockets and switches that once facili-tated now long-forgotten cutting-edge practices.

Offices and other working spaces

Aside from these spaces for teaching, learning and information use, another obvious example of the digitally shaped spaces of the university campuses are the offices that constitute the working environments for academics and profes-sional staff. Perhaps because these spaces tend to be hidden from public view, universities authorities tend to invest less in the bespoke design of offices and working spaces. Nevertheless, there are many examples of campus buildings that fulfil a brief as working environments for digital university work. Deakin University's recently constructed 'Frontage Building' in Melbourne is one such example – a striking design of what the architects describe as 'new generation academic workspaces' that accommodate individual offices alongside open-plan workspaces. This combination of informal and formal meeting space is intended to support increased 'interaction and collaboration' – deliberately supporting the use of portable digital technologies as part of the inherent 'connectivity' of the building use. Here, then, the intention is to infuse university work with the pat-terns of twenty-first century knowledge work – as the architects describe: 'unique to this project is that the interior spaces are more akin to today's workplace environments than traditional academic spaces' (Woods Bagot Architects 2012, n.p.). In the UK, Nottingham University's much vaunted Jubilee campus offers a contrasting take on the twenty-first century working environment – combining landscaped lakeside parks and boulevards with wooden-clad, environmentally-aware office spaces that offset the energy consumption, light and heat emissions of all the digital technology being used within them with the use of renewable energy sources, natural ventilation, lighting sensors and roofing insulated by alpine plants.

Of course, most refurbishments and makeovers of university working spaces are by no means as innovative. More commonly the introduction of information technology from the 1960s onwards has instigated the building of the open, white office space that now characterizes much of the higher education working environment – particularly for professional staff. As Brand (1994) reasons, the growth of information technology-based work was directly responsible for the development of the design of many 'glass-plate' university buildings. These are characterized by open office environments, with raised floors and dropped ceilings clad with acoustic tiles to accommodate cabling, bundles of wires, cable trays, ventilation ducts and so on. These offices are housed in soulless, sealed buildings with overloaded air conditioning, double-glazed windows and florescent strip lighting. As Brand (1994, p.170) observes, the architectural approach to this could be seen to be little more than 'hang a curtain wall of glass on the outside of your tall fat box, and take a bow' (p.170).

Indeed, the realities of working in some of these environments are far removed from the clean, tidy lines of architectural plans and project briefs. The temporary, transient nature of university open-plan offices often makes for a decidedly messy working environment. The tendency to 'hot-desk' results in various traces of previous occupants, from the desktop detritus of the dried-up pot plant to the random assortment of paperclips and unidentifiable data cables. Laptop computers, smart phones, e-book readers and the variety of personal digital divides that individuals tend to carry around with them, all require power points to charge, leaving the floors of these spaces strewn with a tangle of adapters, plugs, power strips and cabling. The lack of available storage space leaves little room for books, paper, stationary and all other material artefacts that university work still requires. Smart lighting is often anything but smart – usually stuck in a state of being either fully 'on' or fully 'off'. These are spaces that are dominated by the sound, heat and smell of printers and photocopiers – housed alongside people's work stations and desks. Moreover, the immersion of people working on-screen makes for a stilted, stultifying atmosphere. Workers in these spaces are reluctant to break from their own digital bubble and make extraneous noise for fear of breaking the concentration and immersion of their nearby colleagues. These are often far from the buzzy, collegial, collaborative spaces that they may have been designed to be.

These constraints and compromises are also apparent in the majority of older 'closed' office spaces across universities where digital technologies have been inserted in and around the existing working environments. It is rare to see an office space on campus that is not both stuffed full of paper (in the form of books, box files and stacks of photocopies) as well as dominated by a desktop computer. Similar to our earlier descriptions of libraries and teaching spaces, a variety of digital technologies are crammed into the working spaces of academics and professional staff in an ad hoc manner. These technologies are sometimes accompanied by appropriately designed furniture (ergonomically designed chairs, wrist supports, adequately proportioned desks and so on), but often not. Indeed, working with and around digital technologies in 'found' office spaces often involves a number of physical and spatial discomforts.

The nether regions of the campus

Digital technologies are now embedded (or at least have been 'inserted') in all aspects of the contemporary university environment. This is perhaps most noticeable in the public spaces of the university – i.e. the foyers, corridors, plazas and receptions. These spaces are often populated by digital display screens offering useful advice or else promotional messages to those who are passing through. Some of these spaces invite forms of digital interaction (for example, through touch screens), while many offer wireless connection to the internet. Aesthetically, digital technologies and digital cultures are often most visible in the design of student unions, student activities centres, student commons and other student spaces – which tend to be regularly refurbished and rebranded to retain relevance to the current cohort of student consumers. These spaces will often appropriate the language and grammar of digital technology – featuring hubs, nodes and portals. Accommodating digital technology use and connectivity has also become a key element of arranging and promoting student accommodation. Now student halls of residence and accommodation blocks will be defined as much in terms of their digital facilities and connectivity, as their bathrooms, kitchens and bedrooms. 'Free' and fast internet connectivity coupled with digital entertainment options are now far more of a selling point than en-suite bathroom facilities or kitchen appliances.

Yet perhaps the most significant material features of the contemporary 'digital' university environment are the least visible to most people who populate campus spaces. All universities – however newly built – are home to a considerable material infrastructure that facilities the apparently immaterial use of digital technologies on campus. Universities are home to multiple server rooms and even server buildings. Roofs of buildings will house a variety of antennae and dishes. Above all are the hundreds of miles of cabling required to facilitate all the forms of digital technology use that are taking place within the university. As Blum (2012) observes, the internet is not located in a cloud – it is hardly wire *less*. Indeed, as Adrian Mackenzie (2010, p.64) continues:

> While the notion of wireless networks implies that there are fewer wires, it could easily be argued that actually there are more wires. Rather than wireless cities or wireless networks, it might be more accurate to speak of the rewiring of cities through the highly reconfigurable paths of chipsets.

As such, any university will be home to miles of underground tubing and piping that houses a tangle of cables. These will have multiple access points, often unsubtly taking the form of manhole covers and entry panels. The sides of building will sometimes house shiny silver tanks of nitrogen required to prevent moisture from damaging underground lines. Copper and optical fibre cabling will be crammed into the ceilings and floors of building, requiring access points and crawl spaces to facilitate maintenance. Rooms will be home to routers the size of washing machines connected to thick bundles of cables and junction boxes. All of these physical aspects of the digital infrastructure need to be located somewhere on campus. If you take a moment to look, then the university soon reveals itself to be a sprawling 'machine' for digital work and digital life.

Making sense of the materialities of the digital university

These descriptions give some sense of how people, digital artefacts and the built campus environment are materially woven together to make the particular place that is the contemporary 'university'. Of course, the physical infrastructure of bricks, glass, cables and wires could be seen as separate from the people who work and practices that take place within it. It could be reasoned that as long as one can connect a digital device to the internet then one can engage in online learning regardless of one's immediate environment. Yet the descriptions just provided all lend weight to the alternative reading that the physical and social working spaces of the 'university' are in fact deeply entwined with the digital practices and processes of 'higher education'. It could be argued, therefore, that the practices of teaching, learning, researching or administrating with digital technologies take place in conjunction with the material construction of the built environment. In developing a good understanding of the shaping of digital higher education, we need to pay close attention to the influence of the materialities of the university. So what influence do these material constructions of the university have on the use of digital technology?

The symbolic nature of 'digital' architecture

In many ways, universities are not good examples of the adaptability of buildings in the face of technological change. Indeed, it could be argued that the combination of digital change and the institutional nature of universities creates an architectural 'perfect storm' where two immovable objects collide. On one hand, as has just been described, digital technology can be seen as a 'restless, remorseless, destructive' influence on buildings (Brand 1994, p.168) – demanding substantial reshaping of layouts, taking up more space, using more electricity. On the other hand, universities are housed in institutional buildings which (unlike their commercial or domestic counterparts) are especially resistant to change. As Brand (1994, p.7) continues:

> [I]nstitutional buildings act as if they were designed specifically to prevent change for the organization inside and to convey timeless reliability to everyone outside. When forced to change anyway, as they always are, they do so with expensive reluctance and all possible delay. Institutional buildings are mortified by change.

In this sense, it is perhaps unsurprising that the material realities of the digital university are rarely satisfactory or efficient. Indeed, it could be concluded – somewhat cynically – that the primary purpose of many of the university renovations and refurbishments just described is symbolic and expressive rather than substantive. As Nansen et al. (2011, p.695) reason: 'here, the building becomes a site of identity, display, and exchange' – therefore part of constructing the 'story' of what the university is, while making little real difference to what goes on. This is certainly apparent in the university renovations where digital technology increasingly informs the aesthetic and visual appearance and graphic design of higher education environments, while the material substance of the building remains largely unaltered. Take, for instance, the ever-changing student unions and campus centres. These are spaces that are regularly refurbished and rebranded to retain relevance to current student culture – decorated with the latest signs and symbols of the digital age while retaining their long-standing basic forms and functions.

The symbolic value of a high-tech design or renovation is certainly evident in some of the examples of new designs and new buildings previously considered in this chapter. For example, the University of York's official description of its £20 million refurbishment of its main library placed the building's components in a telling order:

> The refurbished Library offers a range of 21st-century technology and media-rich learning, teaching and research environments in proximity to specialist support and physical collections. The ground floor of the Library is also home to the Library Café.

At least the librarians and the book collections are prioritized above the café, although clearly well below '21st-century technology and media-rich learning'. Similarly, Deakin University's new Frontage Building was described officially as 'set to be a world-class educational facility that will create a major impression at the entrance of the University' (Ozler 2012). An even more blatant sense of symbolism is evident in the building of Nottingham's Jubilee Campus – as Peter Wilson (2008) observes:

> As part of its expansion, the University of Nottingham wanted to create distinctive images of the institution's modernity, symbols that could feature strongly on prospectuses and other marketing material. It is in this context that [the] buildings should be considered. With 35,000 staff and students spread over four campuses in its home city, and with other campuses in China and Malaysia, the University of Nottingham is ranked fifth in the table of UK universities for its number of overseas students. The expansion of its Jubilee Campus is primarily aimed at attracting top-flight staff, students and investment from this global market.

Deliberately scripted spaces

There is certainly an element of truth in the notion that buildings are constructed (and later renovated) to reinforce cultural messages, and to create and communicate meaning (O'Toole and Were 2008). Yet, regardless of these symbolic functions, university architectures should also be seen as playing a key role in the performance of digital higher education. These built environments all provide a material context within which digital technologies are used, and digital practices emerge. It could therefore be argued that some of these buildings and spaces are designed deliberately to interpolate certain digital performances and shape their execution. Indeed, Mattern (2007, p.283) highlights the disciplinary qualities of architecture, pointing out how physical space can be designed to enforce 'appropriate' behaviour and ensure that people 'will properly perform'. As such, we need to also consider the 'stage and script' of university buildings, rooms and other spaces in relation to the types of digital practices they are intended to instigate and encourage.

This raises the idea of the built university environment as a 'scripted space' designed to shape digital actions along certain lines. As Andersen and Pold (2011) have argued, the architectural layout of a space, alongside the positioning of digital hardware, and the acoustic and lighting designs all contribute to an intended (or at least anticipated) set of digital practices. In some instances, these scripts can be deliberately controlling – such as the 'ergonomic control' (Klein 2004) implicit in the design of seating or table space to encourage or discourage the use of a laptop computer, the deliberate positioning of power points in public spaces and so on. Of course, this control and manipulation is often apparent to anyone newly entering the space, and often freely entered into and experienced as a sort of 'happy imprisonment' (Klein 2004). However, often these scripts contain an element of exclusivity – requiring passwords to log-on to wireless networks, placing limitations on the time and space that can be devoted to digital practices. In this sense, these spaces become more apparent to those who inhabit them:

> Obviously, a scripted space is experienced in many different ways, but an important aspect is the feeling that something is going on behind the facade and that there are powers controlling and structuring what is seen and experienced. The immediate experience of the urban is disturbed by the feeling that there is something unreadable, but still scripted, programming the space.
>
> (Andersen and Pold 2011, pp.113–114)

The unintended structuring of digital action

Of course, this notion of university spaces as being scripted for digital technology use applies only to the newly designed or recently renovated aspects of the campus. For the most part, the 'found' spaces where the majority of teaching, working and social interactions take place within a university do not imbue any deliberate script intended to support particular forms of digital technology use. Although these spaces have been described at various points in this chapter as ad hoc and unplanned, this is not to deny their influence on what takes place within them. These found spaces therefore shape and influence digital practices in a variety of unintended (and often obtrusive) ways – what can be described as the unintended structuring of digital action.

Indeed, this chapter has described how many university spaces (teaching rooms, office space and so on) take the 'found' form of messy, cramped, compromised arrangements of new digital technologies being continually 'added' to the remnants of previous generations of technology use. As with the deliberately scripted spaces described above, these found arrangements should be seen as having a degree of influence in shaping particular kinds of digital technology use. These influences were obviously not intended in the original design of the spaces, yet have cumulated over the years as spaces have adapted and evolved to the changing activities and practices of those working within them.

At the very least, the examples highlighted in this chapter suggest a general 'anachronistic latency' that characterizes many material spaces within a university – their slowness 'to respond to the stimulus of media and technological stuff, which strain against its obduracy' (Nansen et al. 2011, p.694). There is clearly a mismatch between the relatively stable materiality of the physical university environment in comparison to the fast-moving, shifting digital cultures of work, teaching and research. Thus the main issue underlying the influence of the materialities of higher education on digital technology is as much temporal as it is spatial – especially with regards to the permanence of the built environment that inverts the dictum of 'form follows function'. Instead, much of what takes place within universities could be seen as a case of digital function following material form. As Stewart Brand (1994, p.2) concludes, 'buildings loom over us and persist beyond us. They have the perfect memory of materiality . . . they are designed not to adapt.'

On one hand, this can be seen as an expected feature of architecture and materiality in general – much of what has been discussed in this chapter are not observations unique to higher education settings per se. On the other hand, the lack of planning and forethought that goes into the messy 'found' environments that shape much digital technology use in universities could be said to betray the implicit realities of digital higher education. These spaces certainly contrast with the corporate spin and institutional symbolism of the high-tech, high-functioning campus. Instead these are spaces that make digital technology use an often difficult, awkward, clumsy and compromised experience – therefore reflecting the general 'grind' of the realities of digital education. In other words, these spaces could be seen as difficult, dysfunctional contexts for difficult, dysfunctional work – starkly belying the rhetoric of digital higher education that continues to be produced outside of the university campus.

Conclusions

The material features of educational institutions are a rarely considered aspect of 'digital' education, yet should be seen as an integral element of any analysis of higher education and technology. In contrast to the 'wireless', 'placeless', 'weightless' rhetoric of the digital age, this chapter has shown how the increased use of digital technologies in higher education actually involves more 'stuff' – be it cabling and power points, walls, ceilings and glass frontages, elaborate furniture, new rooms and buildings. Sometimes these material adjustments and reconfigurations are designed and planned well – yet more often digital technologies are inserted into universities in clumsy and awkward ways. This is the case with newly designed and long-standing 'found' architectures. Indeed, many of the newly designed and renovated examples of university architecture could be said to follow architectural fashion rather than educational needs. We should not be simply berating universities for failing to make substantial organizational or cultural reconstructions alongside the frenzy of new designs and new buildings that has seized the university sector over the past few decades. As Rachel Hurdley (2010, p.46) contends,

> whilst the increased 'mass' of higher education might demand a different architecture in its institutions, as might changing lifestyle and academic work patterns, my argument is that the 'new' architecture that is taking place in higher education is not a response to the specific requirements of academia.

The materialities of the contemporary university therefore need to be seen as a key component of the unsatisfactory nature of much digital technology use in higher education. This is perhaps inevitable given the intransient nature of any built environment:

> [A]lmost no buildings adapt well. They're designed not to adapt: also budgeted and financed not to, maintained not to, constructed not to, administered not to, maintained not to, regulated and taxed not to, even remodelled not to. But all buildings (expect monuments) adapt anyway, however poorly, because the usages in and around them are changing constantly.
>
> (Brand 1994, p.2)

Thus, it is perhaps to be expected that contemporary university spaces are a messy testament to the history of technology use that has evolved within them. As Brand (1994, p.2) continues, buildings have 'the perfect memory of materiality'. Thus it is in many ways understandable that universities are an 'archive' of past and present digital processes and practices (Rao 2009). One should not overlook the mess of digital infrastructures within universities – the clutter of digital higher education – most notably in the form of obsolesced machines, old cables, mysterious boxes in the wall and useless adapters. These assemblages of past technologies are emblematic of the digital histories and cultures that shape the present.

Of key importance to this book's wider analysis, however, is the interplay between the messy realities of the relations of people, media and architecture – not least how the material aspects of digital higher education correspond with the shaping and control of individual action. Here, this chapter has noted how the built environment of the digital university is both a 'manifestation and influence on our cultures, social structures, sense of agency, identity and power structures' (O'Toole and Were 2008, p.631). As Hurdley (2010) reminds us, the spatial arrangement and built environments of university campuses are 'notable for the[ir] sociopolitical designs' – part of the 'traditional cartography of power' in which actions are controlled and 'conventional, institutionalized thinking' is embodied and enacted. If we extend La Corbusier's notion of the building as a 'machine for living', then the machine of the university is clearly a manifestation of culture, both of the organization and of the broader social system. As O'Toole and Were (2008, p.619) continue:

> Mumford suggested that 'the machine cannot be divorced from its larger social pattern; for it is this pattern that gives it meaning and purpose'. In a factory, for example, there is a system of discipline, of rules, of politics in the traditional sense. The forms of machines help enforce these rules: they suggest the easiest possibilities to those who use them. They mediate between the people who make the rules and the people who have to follow them. The social structures that influence and are influenced by the material culture and space are in juxtaposition to the human need to protect personal space and maintain identity.

So, if there is one conclusion to be taken forward from this chapter, it is that the politics of space and place is a crucial element of developing fairer forms of digital higher education. This is clearly a consideration that needs further exploration in our final analysis. Indeed, we are now in a position of being able to move on from the past four chapters' examination of specific aspects of higher education in the digital age. The final two chapters of this book now take us back out into the wider concerns of making full sense of contemporary higher education, with the ultimate aim of adjusting, improving and thinking 'otherwise'. What do we now know about higher education and digital technology, and most importantly, what can we do about it?

Part III

So what now?

Chapter 7

Looking back

Making sense of universities in the digital age

Introduction

Some readers may have found this book's portrayal of digital technology and higher education a little disorientating. The critical picture emerging from the past six chapters is certainly at odds with the upbeat, 'can-do', 'what-if?' ways that education and technology is usually discussed. Indeed, debates about 'ed-tech' tend to be treated as an opportunity to consider possibilities and potentials, and to wallow in the apparent unknown-ness of it all. This attitude was captured neatly in Wendy Hamer's reflection on the future of news journalism in the digital age: 'eventually something will crawl out of the primordial soup . . . we don't know what it is but isn't it fantastic to be in this soup?' (cited in Haigh 2012, n.p.). Even within the beleaguered newspaper, music and book publishing industries, Hamer is by no means alone in her sense of wonder and anticipation. So if people in even these professions are able to imagine the possibilities of a brighter future, then why cannot the most critically minded of educationalists follow suit? In this sense, I am well aware of what some readers might be thinking at this point in the book . . . Is it really *that* difficult to be a little more open-minded and hopeful about what the future holds? . . . Just *why* do you find it so hard to generate a modicum of enthusiasm for what the digital future holds for universities?

While there is little pleasure to be taken from being relentlessly negative, it still seems that a pessimistic perspective is the best way of making full sense of digital technology and higher education – particularly if one is concerned with the societal and cultural value of public education. If nothing else, a pessimistic view remains true to the realities of what has *actually* taken place with regards to higher education and digital technology over the past thirty years (to be blunt, things have clearly *not* been transformed or improved by digital technology so far, so why should we expect anything different in the near future?). Moreover – and most importantly – getting sucked into the 'soup' of digital hype, hope and speculation almost inevitably distracts from the many injustices that run throughout digital higher education. Indeed, this book's pessimism has highlighted a litany of conflicts, contradictions and compromises that demand *immediate* attention if the quality and character of our universities are not to be debased irrevocably.

Although it might not be fashionable to admit it, this rescue mission cannot be achieved by simply daydreaming of potential digital salvation. Instead, we need to retain our critical facilities and begin to consider ways of fighting back against the clearly unsatisfactory realities of higher education in the digital age. This chapter therefore concerns itself with reconsidering what the main underlying problems are with digital technology and higher education. We should then be in a good position to give serious thought to how things might be otherwise.

What has been found, and what does it mean?

This book has reached a series of conclusions about the complicated and compromised realities of higher education and digital technology. Looking back over the past six chapters, the following recurring themes and issues are perhaps worthy of highlighting:

- Digital technologies are a deeply embedded element of contemporary higher education – you cannot hope to understand higher education without paying serious attention to the varied uses of digital technology across the sector. Conversely, you cannot fully understand digital technology use in higher education without paying serious attention to the wider linkages, shifts and pressures on the context of the contemporary university. These include: globalized flows of staff and students, finance, information and culture; the demands of global economics as conveyed through the actions of employers and governments; new forms of capitalism that are 'immaterial' and 'cognitive' in nature; the growing privatization and commercialization of many higher education products and processes; the influence of managerialist forms of organization and governance throughout universities.
- Universities – in organizational and physical form – are increasingly based upon digital systems of regulation, management and control. These systems increasingly shape what it is to 'work' within the contemporary university – be it in terms of time, social relations, communication or the form and function of the built environment. Digital technologies – despite their connotations of individual freedom and personalization – are most often associated with a 'cellular individualization' – linked with a concentration of power at the centre, rather than a dispersal of power to the edges.
- Digital technologies fit uneasily and awkwardly with the contours of higher education (be they material, cultural, philosophical) – which have often built up over decades, if not centuries, and are understandably resistant to change. More often than not, digital technologies find a 'fit' with the tacit 'grammar' of higher education that is based increasingly around the rise of 'new managerial' techniques of measurement, monitoring, comparison and evaluation. As such, digital technologies are often encountered within universities in 'institutional' roles e.g. gathering data, allowing the storage and transfer of instructional content, synchronous and asynchronous communication.

In this way, digital technologies are associated closely with accountability, productivity, monitoring, measuring, surveillance and what can be termed 'performativity'.

Alongside these issues and themes, it could be argued that there is not much 'new' about the ways in which digital technologies are being used in higher education. On the one hand, it could be reasonable to conclude that digital technology changes little for the better. It could be reasoned that digital technology simply amplifies, intensifies and accelerates already existing trends – be it the exploitation of workers or the instrumentalization of teaching and learning. These are not new developments per se, but are often extended and accelerated through digital means. The clichéd conclusion of 'old wine in new bottles' certainly remains of relevance here. As such, none of the technological 'solutions' that are currently being touted around higher education – not least recent enthusiasms for an 'iPad for every student', 'flipped classrooms' or 'massive open online courses' – are likely to alter substantially the wider failings of the business of contemporary higher education. They are most likely to lead simply to more of the same.

On the other hand, it would be misleading to claim that there is absolutely *nothing* new associated with the increased use of digital technologies. Certainly, this book has been littered with examples of practices and processes that would not be possible without digital technology. Many of these 'new' features of digital education relate to the increased connectivity that digital technologies afford. Portable personalized technologies mean that one can be 'always on' regardless of time or place. Moreover, when using a networked technology one is certainly far more visible to far more people in a far more instantaneous manner than ever before. This obviously alters the relationships that people have with other people, with places and with time. It makes increasingly less sense to talk about the 'university' and 'home', 'work time' and 'leisure time'. Digital technologies clearly have had a pervasive influence on social arrangements and social relations. The mistake that many commentators make, however, is to imagine these changes to be almost exclusively beneficial (if not empowering) to the individual user. As we have seen throughout this book, the realities are far from this simple. The 'benefits' of digital technology use depend very much on who and where you are within the hierarchy of higher education.

Unpacking digital higher education: key themes and tensions

The time has come to make better sense of the different forms of digital higher education reviewed so far in this book. Clearly, much of what has been highlighted over the past six chapters relates to the generally dulled character and diminished circumstances of universities as organizations. Despite the brilliant and sharp minds of many of the people working in higher education, as a whole universities are not the most brilliant or sharpest of organizations. A lot of what has been highlighted in this book could be traced back to the general dysfunctional nature of universities, which is tempered only by their ability to somehow continue in an ad hoc, haphazard manner in the face of seemingly insurmountable change. Yet, much of what has been described in this book could be seen as going beyond the day-to-day dysfunction of the university. There are a number of critical issues and entrenched themes that underpin the narrow and pernicious uses of digital technology in higher education that need identifying and isolating. If we are to stand a chance of resisting the currently detrimental forms of digital technology at play within contemporary higher education, then it is important to be clear on what these wider issues are.

Power and control

First and foremost, much of this book highlights the importance of power in making sense of digital technology. Digital education should therefore be seen as a significant carrier, conveyor and creator of power relations within higher education. Some of the key contradictions that run throughout contemporary forms of higher education relate to imbalances of what people have the capacity to do (and not do) through digital technologies, as well as what is permitted and what is prevented. This was apparent, for example, throughout Chapter 3. Here we saw how the implementation of VLEs in university courses is not primarily concerned with support or stimulating learning per se, but is linked with processes of social control. The same can be said for business decision systems, management information systems or research management systems. These are all systems that serve to reinforce routines i.e. the established ways of doing things and the established hierarchical relationships between people and different parts of the university organization. Digital technologies should therefore be understood as an important means through which relations of domination and subordination are enforced and extended in universities.

Most significantly, we have seen many examples throughout this book of how these digitally mediated power relations are distributed unequally. While popular assumptions persist that digital technology can have a 'centrifugal' effect on relations of authority and control within universities, much of what we have seen during the past six chapters would suggest that it is mainly 'centripetal' i.e. leading to a centralization of power rather than a more democratic redistribution of power to those previously less powerful. Indeed, it could be argued that the increased use of digital technology in higher education serves mainly to increase the ability of dominant powerful groups to control the actions of others. This control is achieved primarily by influencing, shaping or even determining the majority's wants, preferences, expectations of what is possible and what is preferable.

Seen in these terms, it is clearly misleading to continue to frame digital technology as unproblematically increasing the power of *all* individuals within a university context to act. Instead, as Holloway (2002, p.28) reminds us, any increase in power is embedded in the fragmentation of social relations: 'our capacity to do is always an interlacing of our activity with the previous or present activity of others. Our capacity to do is always the result of the doing of others.' Digital technology is more accurately seen as part of ongoing conflicts between those who hold 'power over' the actions of those whom 'power is done to'. In this sense, the politics of digital higher education are, as Tim Jordan (1999, p.211) describes it, 'an elaborate dance between individual empowerment and elite domination'.

Crucially, many of the forms of digital technology outlined in this book could be seen as supporting the maintenance of existing patterns of domination through the largely non-conflictory manufacturing of individual 'consent to their own subordination' (Delgardo 1993, p.674). Indeed, as Steven Lukes (1974/2005) reminds us, the most effective forms of power are often those that individuals perceive as enabling changes that are in their interests. We have seen how digital technologies embody what Nicholas Gane (2012, p.625) terms 'underlying governmental logics of neoliberalism' i.e. new regimes of accountability and internal controls in the form of monitoring techniques. Key here, then, is the extent to which digital technologies function as a means to restrict the power of less dominant social groups within higher education without them even realizing it i.e. students, academic staff involved in teaching, junior and/or fixed-term researchers, middle-managers, administrators and professional staff. These are people for whom prescribed forms of digital technology use are 'virtually mandatory' elements of their university work (see Shelton 2014). We therefore need to pay serious attention towards the extent to which these 'new' educational technologies are explicitly disempowering and restrictive for all but an elite minority.

There is much to suggest that many of the digital reforms of university organizations serve to restrict and disempower individuals along managerial lines. As Waring and Skoumpopoulou's (2013, p. 1378) study of the digitally driven reorganization of one UK university concludes, the institution-wide introduction of online administration systems can have a subtle and wide-reaching influence on universities, legitimizing managerialism and engendering a sense of powerlessness amongst professional and academic staff:

> Administrative management now appear to have increasing power within the university, and from the perspective of many academic staff, resistance appears futile. This power is evident as managers introduce new information technology applications to monitor and manage academic funding applications. The university is also piloting the use of an information technology system to manage academic research outputs. Little consultation has taken place with academic staff, and once again the rhetoric is around efficiency and effectiveness.

These perceptions of regulation, restructure and the futility of resistance run counter to usual rhetoric of individually empowering digital technology. Indeed, the forms of virtual system outlined in Chapter 3, and the associated working conditions for staff and students alike examined in Chapters 4 and 5, all reflect what

Bauman terms the 'managerial revolution mark two'. The self-surveillance, self-reporting and self-regulation that many digital technologies are now entwined with could be seen as part of an 'IKEA' style of domination and control i.e. where individuals are expected to construct and maintain their own structures of subordination:

> [T]he managers having discovered a much better (less costly as well as less burdensome and unwieldy, and potentially more profitable) recipe for control and domination: hiring out managerial duties to the managed themselves, transferring the task of keeping them in line from debit to credit, from liabilities to assets, from costs to gains – by 'subsidiarizing' that tasks to those at the receiving end of the operation. This is something that IKEA is famous for – leaving the assembly of factory-produced elements to clients paying for the privilege of doing the job, instead of being remunerated for its performance – but it is a principle every more widely deployed in shaping the present-day patters of the domination/subordination relationship.
>
> (Bauman and Lyon 2013, p.140)

Status and class

This reading of digital higher education in terms of power, control and self-regulation continues onto the crucial (but often overlooked) issue of class and digital technology. The importance of class is easily overlooked in the individualized and meritocracized discourses that have captured popular, political and academic imaginations from the 1990s onwards. Within the discourses of aspiration – where 'anyone' can succeed with the right tools and the right mindset – issues such as class are rendered redundant. This is even more applicable to discussions of higher education – where 'everyone' is assumed to be in a (relatively) well-paid, secure occupation, or well on the way to getting one. However, as has been suggested throughout this book, digital technology use in higher education is clearly associated with some social interests and groups benefiting over others.

Indeed, the social groups that appear to benefit most from the use of digital technology in education could be said to reflect the interests of the privileged interests outlined in Chapters 3, 4 and 5 i.e. the economic and technological elites associated with neoliberalism, the 'new' economy, creative capitalism and so on. It is reasonable to conclude, therefore, that digital education is similarly 'embedded into the antagonisms of capitalist society . . . a class-structured, segmented, stratified social space' (Fuchs 2008, p.346). As such, discourses of providing *all* individuals with the skills, competences and aptitudes to thrive in the new economy are clearly disingenuous. These class divisions are clearly the case when it comes to university workers' experiences of the digitization of their professional practices and responsibilities. Similarly, in terms of university students, it makes little sense for elite interests to support the development of a majority of empowered, innovative, entrepreneurial, self-directed and creatively 'disruptive' individuals – even if they are graduates or post-graduates who have worked their way through all of the hoops and hurdles of the formal education system. Not all university academics, professional staff or students are the same.

As Alex Means (2011, p.225) contends, contemporary capitalism requires higher education to produce 'a small and manageable core of highly skilled workers', alongside a majority of people who remain docile, subordinate and ultimately exploited by dominant interests. In national university systems containing up to 50 per cent of the population of young people, higher education is therefore required to fulfil a rigid sorting function. We have seen much throughout this book to suggest that digital technologies play a key role in this stratification. Indeed, for both university students and workers, digital technologies can be seen as a ready means of maintaining stratification between different classes. Of course, this needs to be seen within the new fragmented class structures of contemporary society – what Andre Gorz (1982) termed 'the end of the working class'. Class has certainly been a shifting concept throughout the past thirty years – with traditional assumptions of stratification in terms of a person's position in the labour process and the status associated with a person's occupation no longer holding true. Standing (2011), for example, identifies at least seven groups within the contemporary structure of class:

- elite: small number of 'absurdly rich' (i.e. the top one per cent);
- salariat: stable, full-time employment with pensions, holidays, state benefits – concentrated in large corporations, government agencies, public administration (including civil servants);
- proficians (professional/technician): those with bundles of skills that they can market, earning high incomes on contract, acting as consultants or independent own-account workers;
- manual employees: industrial labour;
- precariat;
- unemployed;
- socially-ill misfits/underclass.

A critical element of Standing's analysis is the number of university graduates who are now being prepared for existences outside of the elite, salariat or profician classes, and instead within what can be terms the 'precariat'. These are temporary, fragmented, careerless jobs – leaving people experiencing little or no control over any aspects of their labour i.e. in terms of skill development, skill use, time, timing or intensity. The precariat can be characterized as lacking various forms of labour security – be it in terms of protection against dismissal, job security, opportunities to gain skills or a stable income. Crucially, this class is left lacking a secure work-based identity or employment narrative, 'without tradition of social memory, a feeling they belong to an occupational community steeped in stable practices, codes of ethics and norms of behaviour, reciprocity and fraternity' (Standing 2011, p.12).

Using digital technology in the ways that they are, it could be argued that many university students are getting good practical experience of the skills and dispositions required for the part-time, precarious work that they may well be graduating into. A flexible engagement with education through LMSs, MOOCs and the like, is perfect preparation for the flexible labour relations of twenty-first century capitalism – which are similarly short-term, temporary and outsourced. Indeed, these digitally regulated working conditions are being experienced within these students' universities by the administrators, managers and teaching staff who find themselves labouring precariously in the higher education sector. When a student is 'learning' through watching video clips and participating in discussion forums, or an administrator is dealing with an email inbox on a Sunday evening at home, it is hard to argue against the correspondences between digital technology use in higher education and the disjointed working patterns of twenty-first century capitalism.

Of course, it is possible to see these working conditions and class formations in positive terms of flexibility and individual freedom from the rigidity of 'stable' employment. It is possible to see the 'precariatization' of graduate labour (and the university education required to get you there) in positive terms: 'romantic free spirit[s] who reject norms of the old working class steeped in stable labour, as well as the bourgeois materialism of those in salaried 'white-collar' jobs' (Standing 2011, p.9). However, there is a fine line between becoming one of the minority of creative 'profician' classes (such as designers, programmers, professional artists and performers) who lead a productive and lucrative project-orientated existence, and the exploitative temporary jobs and internships that rather more graduates may eventually find themselves competing for. In class terms, universities could be said to be preparing many more students for a lifetime of alienation and instrumentality, a limited range of rights and options, and a certain 'drift towards opportunism' (Standing 2011, p.12). There is little to suggest that digital technologies are doing anything to counter this trend.

Privatization and commodification

Digital technology is not only associated with maintaining divisions between dominant elite and subordinate majority groups. It is also linked with the exploitation of public education for private gain. While not always obvious, many of this book's chapters have reflected the increased presence of privatization values throughout the digitalization of education. As the past four chapters demonstrate, digital processes and practices are often implicit in the reframing and repositioning of public higher education into the domain of private interests. These privatizations are manifest in at least two distinct ways. First, digital technologies are implicated in what Richard Hatcher (2000) calls the 'endogenous privatization' of education i.e. strengthening the notion of internal markets based around increased choice and diversity of provision, alongside competitive forms of consumption. In this sense, digital technologies support a plurality of educational provision that contributes to the shifting of higher education activities 'closer to those of the private sector or even move them fully into that sector' (Crouch 2011, p.71).

Second, all these digital technologies are also implicated in what Hatcher terms 'exogenous privatization' i.e. enhancing and extending the importance of non-state and private actors as education providers. Indeed, one of the clear 'digitizations' of higher education described in this book is the reconstitution of education into forms that are reducible, quantifiable and ultimately contractible out to various actors outside of the educational community (Maguire et al. 2011). It is therefore unsurprising that a number of powerful private concerns are to be found (often surreptitiously) in the various digitizations described throughout this book – from the multi-billion dollar concerns of Google, Pearson, Serco, Microsoft and Facebook, to a range of more locally focused business interests. Thus regardless of their origins, the increasing use of digital technology in higher education is clearly linked with the increased 'dominance of public life by the giant corporation' (Crouch 2011, p.viii). As Picciano and Spring (2013) have argued, digital technologies are now a key vehicle for the profit-driven interests of the 'educational-industrial complex'.

The idea of private interests bringing their 'can-do' faith in technological innovation to bear on the beleaguered and sluggish university sector is clearly seductive for many people. As Sebastian Thrun, credited with the popularization of the MOOC concept and co-founder of online learning company Udacity Inc. bluntly put it: '[Higher] education is broken. Face it . . . it is so broken at so many ends, it requires a little bit of Silicon Valley magic' (cited in Wolfson 2013). Yet one of the major outcomes of this privileging of market organization within digital education is the increased diversion of education into a commodity state i.e. framing education processes and practices into the 'market form' of something that has calculable and quantifiable value, and that is therefore exchangeable (Appadurai 2005). It seems clear that one of the consequences of many of these digital technologies is the reconfiguration of educational practices and relations into forms that can be quantified and exchanged. For example, Chapter 3 illustrated how 'virtual' systems permit the intensification of capital accumulation in education by fragmenting various education services and aspects of educational work into commodity-like units and tasks. As Vincent Mosco (2004, p.135) argues, this commodification is greatly facilitated by digital 'opportunities to measure and monitor, package and repackage'. As we saw in Chapters 3, 4 and 5, all of these processes are supported ably by the digital systems that underpin university work and study.

Changing values and character of university study and university work

This commodification, it can be argued, is also associated with more insidious shifts in the values of higher education. In this sense, we also need to consider the clear but subtle devaluation of the 'character' of higher education – a less tangible notion than inequality or power, but nonetheless important. In this sense, the digital technologies reviewed over the past four chapters could all be said to convey and enforce a limited set of meanings relating to the nature and form of educational 'work' – be it the nature of learning or teaching, questions over the content of curricula, academic research or the administration, management and governance of the university institution. Most important are the links between digital technology use and the shifting understandings of the human relationships that underpin this work.

For example, digital technologies could be seen as infusing spaces traditionally intended for the maintenance of public education and the common good with individualized discourses – what Bauman (2001, p.49) terms as 'the concerns and preoccupations of individuals *qua* individuals'. Tellingly, many of the forms of digital technology use reviewed over the past four chapters maintain an illusion that work and study is taking place on a collective, communal basis while at the same time promising highly individualized forms of 'engagement', 'participation' and 'empowerment'. As Maraizzi (1994/2011, p.123) observes, one of the key paradoxes of these types of neoliberal ideology is their ability to 'make of individualism a collective value producing a feeling of supra-personal belonging'. Yet if studying for a degree or working for a university institution is viewed predominantly in terms of the individual and their maximized competitive advantage, then the argument can be made that educational or professional actions are made *less* meaningful in a moral or ethical sense. In particular, the potential of university-based work or university-based study to have any collective, communal empathy is dramatically reduced and degraded. As Guy Standing (2011, p.23) concludes:

> [A] good society needs people to have empathy, a capacity to project one-self into another's situation [but] feelings of empathy and competition are in common tension. People in incipient competition conceal from others knowledge, information, contacts and resources, in case revealing then would take away a competitive edge. Fear of failure, or being able to active only a limited status, easily leads to disavowal of empathy.

These latter points lead on to the correspondences between digital technology and the altered emotional aspects of study and/or work within universities. In particular, the flexibility and contingency associated with digital higher education could be said to induce an insecurity that leads less to opportunities, and more to 'situations that can only be described as alienated, anomic, anxious and prone to anger' (Standing 2011, p.25). Digital technologies could be said to mitigate against the building of anything permanent, or the establishment of lasting, meaningful structures and networks. As a result, 'reciprocities become fragile' (Standing 2011, p.22), and there is a moral debasing of people's actions and attitudes towards each other – not least in terms of a lack of solidarity and the diminishment of a communal ethic:

[P]olicies promoting labour flexibility erode processes of relational and peer-group interaction that are vital for reproducing skills and constructive attitudes to work. If you expect to change what you are doing at almost any time, to change 'employer' at short notice, to change colleagues, and above all to change what you call yourself, work ethics become constantly contestable and opportunistic.

(Standing 2011, p.23)

In this sense, we need to consider how the commodification of university study and work through various digital means might result in a cheapening of collective, public values – thereby altering the spirit of higher education. The increased mediation of academic, administrative and pedagogic work through digital systems could be seen as lessening many of the informal instances of communication and information sharing that underpin any shared sense of community, collegiality and *espirit de corps* between a group of people. Moreover, these assemblages of digital tools and applications could be said to alter the conditions of these activities from meaningful 'work' to less meaningful 'labour'. As Ron Barnett (2011) – drawing on Hannah Arendt – observes, 'bureaucracy calls for *labour* whereas the authentic work characteristics of academic life is *work*'. Many of the digital systems and practices outlined in this book lean firmly towards the former status of 'labour' rather than the latter status of 'work'.

Similarly, the disembodied and dematerialized forms of technology-based practice described over the past four chapters could all be said to involve the experiencing of higher education on less intimate grounds. Joel Spring (2012), for example, argues that the increased use of digital technology in educational settings encourages the formation of a 'digital mind-set', where most elements of the education system are visualized in terms of being composed of data rather than personal relations. In this sense, we should not overlook the capacity of these digital technologies to 'quantify and instrumentalize' interpersonal relations (Gregg 2011). As the examples of the VLE, LMS and MOOC all demonstrate, digital technologies can easily be used to frame the relationships between teachers and students in terms of finite services or contracts rather than sustained human interaction.

Similarly, the 'total pedagogization of society' or 'social factory' connotations of digital technology highlighted in Chapters 4 and 5 illustrate how technology marginalizes, devalues and degrades much of what university students and university teachers should be doing. These technologies are designed to value educational work that is 'recordable' i.e. subject to being digitally captured or represented. There is no room, for example, for the recording of intellectual tasks pursued for their own intrinsic usefulness or interest (such as wider reading, cogitating, going off on tangents). There is little or no recognition of the non-instructional elements of being a tutor – for example, in terms of pastoral care or basic forms of sociability with students.

Often the values implicit in these digital processes and practices centre on issues of trust and respect. McKenna and Hughes (2013), for example, offer a telling reflection on the values implicit in the use of plagiarism detection software. These include: a changed relationship in terms of the trust relationship between students and teachers; the increased sense of writing as a product; the reframing of plagiarism as deriving solely from the students' actions; and a view of writing that excluded texts that are multimodal, hypertextual or dialogic. Similarly, Bronwyn Williams (2013) sees the underpinning values of course management systems and VLEs as centring on the commodification of knowledge and efficiency, conservative notions of the hierarchical 'classroom', and concerns with control, monitoring and surveillance. Both these commonly used types of digital system convey a set of implicit philosophies and values that might well be at odds with the personal values and professional philosophies of the teachers who are using them.

Of course, much of this digital re-characterization of higher education needs to be contextualized as part of the broader historical shift away from direct social relationships towards indirect social relationships. As Craig Calhoun (1998) has noted, this has come about in part through the increasing role played in society by large-scale markets, impersonal data-driven administrative organizations, communication technologies and ever-more rapid forms of transportation. As Calhoun (1992, pp.211–212) implies, within these wider societal movements, digital technologies are an important means through which the nature and form of interpersonal human relations are remediated and reconstituted: 'indirect relationships do not eliminate direct ones, but they change both their meaning and their sociological significance'. In this sense, one of the potential outcomes of the generally dis-embodied nature of digital higher education is the displacement of substantive social relationships and social practices that traditionally have been seen as constituting 'the university'. A strong argument can therefore be made that in 'the absence of a binding framework such as the face-to-face', university study and work is being experienced in diminished terms of disembodied information transfer rather than richer forms of 'embodied understanding' (Cooper 2002, p.38). This slightly intangible shift is certainly evident in Jonathan Wolff's (2013, n.p.) reflections on the continuing appeal of face-to-face lectures in a world of online courses:

> For as long as the lecture is regarded as better than internet-based learning, it will survive on a substantial scale. And wherein lies its superiority? An interesting question. It is live. It is real. It is put on with you in mind, even if you are one of a large crowd. You experience it with other people. And, perhaps the clincher: it takes place in a university, bursting with life and interesting people who will inspire you in unexpected ways. Somehow live learning can be open and transformative in a way that transcends its educational function.

Overall, then, all these shifts could be said to be contributing to a cumulative 'emptying' of the social and (for want of a better word) 'human' experience of university work and university life. For some critics, this is associated with the reductive tendencies of digital technologies to atomize and fragment human activities to machine-readable forms – thereby losing some of the human essence in this process. For example, it could be argued that many of the digital technologies reviewed in this book distil education processes and practices into series of discrete tasks, thereby 'enclosing people in an entirely commoditized expression of the work to be done' (Menzies 1998, p.92). From this perspective, the partial, segmented, task-orientated, fragmented and discontinuous nature of digital higher education could be seen as a form of 'spiritual alienation' i.e. alienation at the level of meaning, where 'conditions of good work' become detached from the 'conditions of good character' (Sennett 2012). Reflecting on the rise of iTunes U, the University of the People and online degrees, the economist Guy Standing (2011, p.69) also attempted to capture a sense of what is perhaps a shift in the moral character of digital higher education:

> [T]he commodification and standardization is cheapening education, denuding the profession of its integrity and eroding the passing on of informal knowledge. It is strengthening winner-takes-all markets and accelerating the dismantling of an occupational community. A market in human capital will increase emphasis on celebrity teachers and universities, and favour norms and conventional wisdom. The Philistines are not at the gates; they are inside them.

Understanding the 'struggle' of digital higher education

All of these broader concerns – regardless of how esoteric, philosophical or outdated they might appear – point to the fact that digital technology use in universities is something that needs to be problematized and contested along a number of lines. Much of what has just been discussed relates to a struggle over values and principles – not least the 'traditional' values of public higher education (e.g. values of the collective good, equality of opportunity), and the (often) contrasting values of neoliberalism (e.g. values of individualism, market forces, competition). This is not to say that there is a necessarily 'right' or 'wrong' side of this struggle – just that these are conversations that need to take place, and issues that need to be contested. Digital technology cannot continue to be seen as somehow apart from the 'fierce struggle over the control' of higher education (Winner 1998, p.374). Much of what has been discussed in this book points to the need to engage with the politics of higher education and technology. To reiterate a point made at the beginning of this book, digital higher education therefore needs to be seen as a set of struggles that take place across a number of fronts – from the allocation of resources, design of curricula, and working conditions of university employees to the maximizing of profit and attempts to overcome patterns of exclusion. As Andrew Feenberg (1991, p.14) reminds us, 'technology is not destiny but a scene of struggle'.

In this sense, most of the current academic discussions of universities and digital technology are of limited value. Indeed, much of what is currently being 'discussed' and 'debated' within the academic fields of 'educational technology', e-learning and the like, willfully overlooks the current complex politics of digital technology and higher education in the hope that these problems will soon be addressed through technological and computational means. Yet it is not enough to assume, for example, that digital technologies such as social media will empower individuals (be they employees or students) to transcend the hierarchies and structures of institutionalized education. Looking back to Chapter 4, despite the online 'buzz' amongst educational technologists, we cannot assume that 'digital scholarship' and 'open' and 'networked' approaches to academic work will inevitably soon become the norm simply because the technologies exist to support these behaviours. Indeed, as Esposito (2013, n.p) argues, without institutional coercion to do so, most university-based academic researchers and teachers 'seem not to see any clear benefit to move to further technological means or new open practices'. Similarly, most university students are not automatically empowered by the diversification of digital education provision, or the flexible possibilities of online learning systems. Neither are university administrators and professional staff simply assisted by the 'efficiencies' of digital systems and working practices. The assumption within most discussions of educational technology that digital technologies are either exceptionally beneficial, or else largely neutral, is to miss the intensely political nature of their implementation and use.

This is not to 'blame' anyone working in higher education for somehow not recognizing the politics of digital technology. It would be wrong to portray teachers, students, researchers, academics, administrators and the like simply as unwitting victims; as somehow unconscious of the problematic aspects of digital technology use throughout their working lives. Instead, most people are well aware and knowing of the issues highlighted in this book. However, on a day-to-day basis, most people are largely willing to simply 'work with' these constraints, or perhaps 'work around' them in order to get on with the seemingly more important aspects of their work. Thus it would be wrong to dismiss any of the actors involved in operationalizing the conditions of digital higher education outlined in this book as unknowing and unaware. As Jodi Dean (2002, p.5) reflected on the stultifying self-centred and narcissistic nature of digital media use in everyday life, 'people know very well what they are doing, but they do it nevertheless' (thereby offering a neat updating of Marx's original observation that 'they aren't aware of it, but they do it').

Indeed, there is a curious unwillingness within higher education to challenge the idea(s) of 'digital technology'. This is not a topic that generates a lot of conversation in universities. Instead, people tend to 'rub along' with, and 'work around' the inconveniences of digital technology in ways that they might not with other aspects of their work. On one hand, this is undoubtedly a sane and sensible response to take if one simply wants to get on with the 'more important' aspects of university work. On the other hand, it could be argued that many of the neoliberal and managerial agendas that lie beneath some of the most embedded digital systems in higher education rely on the majority deciding to simply 'comply with it . . . or decide that if they can't beat it, they'll join the game' (Bauman and Lyon 2013, p.8). In other words, it could be reasoned that everyone currently involved with universities is complicit in the clearly unsatisfactory circumstances outlined in this book through their passive inaction, if not their active collusion. Thus it can be argued that digital higher education is a struggle that *must* be more vigorously engaged with – however futile any resistance might seem. While 'ordinary' participants in higher education might seem unlikely to be able to construct a wholly satisfactory alternative set of digital arrangements, there surely is enough talent and tenacity to advance 'productive ideas' on how the 'worst effects' of current digital technology 'might be confronted and countered' (Bauman and Lyon 2013, p.3). In short, it seems appropriate for those of us working in and around universities to at least attempt to think 'otherwise' about the constrictions and compromises associated currently with digital higher education.

Conclusions

This is a challenging position to have reached – especially in comparison to the usually upbeat, optimistic sentiments that pervade popular discussions of education and technology. Happily, we have managed to avoid settling upon a 'doomster' dismissal of all things digital. This book is not arguing that the use of digital technology in higher education is wholly detrimental. There are obviously many examples to be found in universities around the world where individuals and groups *are* making genuinely beneficial, empowering and worthwhile uses of digital technologies. However, it is important to recognize these as exceptions to the rule, rather than the norm. For every professor who 'tweets' with a rapt and responsive community of followers, there are a thousand more whose main experience of digital scholarship is the weekly grind of uploading PowerPoint slides to an LMS and attending cursorily to students' forum postings and emails. This book's analysis is by no means anti-technology per se. It is – however – concerned by the forms of digital technology that constitute the mundane mainstream aspects of digital higher education that are all too easy to overlook. We cannot afford to be distracted by the outliers, the 'leading edge', the spectacular digital possibilities. If we do 'take our eye off the ball' in this manner, then we are destined to repeat the perpetual degree of unrealized but unrelenting boosterism outlined at the beginning of this book. Contemporary universities – and those who work within them – deserve a more thorough and exacting analysis.

That said, it is all too easy to apportion 'blame' for the state of digital higher education on wider forces of neoliberalism, corporatization and globalization that are reshaping entire higher education systems. Indeed, the increasingly utilitarian, instrumentalist, economic-led nature of contemporary higher education undoubtedly drives and shapes digital technology use to a great degree. Yet we should also remember that this digital restructuring of universities and university life 'is, at least in part, made possible by the practices and values of faculty and students' (Cantwell 2013, p.156). In other words, an argument can be made that many of the people most disadvantaged by the narrow digital processes and practices are themselves complicit in the perpetuation of these processes and practices. The thousands of blind-copied emails sent on a Sunday evening do not send themselves, neither do these research management systems or VLEs set themselves up. As Cantwell (2013, p.156) continues, 'this invites self-appraisal for those within higher education. To what extent are "we" (those who teach, study and administer in universities) responsible for this?' The final chapter of this book takes this sentiment of self-appraisal a step further. If 'we' are partially responsible for the dismal state of digital technology use across the university sector, then what can 'we' now do about it?

Chapter 8

Looking forward

Reimagining digital technology and the contemporary university

Introduction

This book started by admitting to 'a nagging dissatisfaction with the current state of universities'. Seven chapters later, there has been little evidence to suggest that digital technology offers any sort of silver bullet to the many problems and shortfalls within contemporary higher education. This is not to dismiss digital technology out of hand, but reaching the conclusion that there is much wrong with the uses of digital technology within higher education should not come as a particular surprise (especially given the critical, pessimistic approach that this book has adopted from the outset). Yet, as has been reiterated throughout the past seven chapters, this is not intended to be a *completely* defeatist exercise. All of our critical discussions and bleak analyses must be approached from Gramsci's perspective of being 'a pessimist because of intelligence, but an optimist because of will'. Thus we need to acknowledge that there might be good grounds for optimism buried beneath this book's dissatisfaction, although this may well not be as spectacular or far-reaching as the optimism that usually surrounds educational technology. We must not, then, lose sight of the last question posed towards the end of Chapter 1, i.e. how could the use of digital technologies in higher education be 'otherwise'?

Given all that has been discussed up until this point, now is the time to consider what can be done to counter the disappointing (and, to be blunt about it, destructive) trends identified in this book. How is it possible to think 'otherwise', to construct 'alternatives' and generally fight back against the worst excesses and bleakest effects of digital higher education? By now it should be clear that digital technology – in and of itself – is not likely to change anything solely for the better. There is no straightforward 'technical fix' that is waiting to be developed or discovered. So, rather than continuing to wait in vain for the great technological leap forwards, it makes sense for everyone in higher education to pay serious attention to what kinds of digital higher education might genuinely be achievable. This final chapter therefore addresses the question that arises ultimately from all of this book's analyses so far: if we still do not like what we have at present, then what *can* we realistically hope for in the future, and how might we get it?

Building a better future by ourselves?

It has become fashionable for books of this sort to end by recommending that alternate technologies need to be built – preferably by people and interests that are excluded currently from the processes of mainstream technology design, development and production. One possible suggestion for change, therefore, is that more people working within higher education should get involved in designing and producing their own digital technologies for teaching, learning, administration and research. Instead of struggling with the pre-configured digital tools and applications that are being imposed continually onto university settings, genuine grassroots interest could be nurtured in the co-creation of alternative digital products, processes and practices. In short, mass participation should perhaps be encouraged in the development of 'digital technology *for* university staff *by* university staff'. Only then might the 'disruptive' and democratizing possibilities of digital technology use that are promised so widely stand a chance of actually being realized in practice.

Conclusions such as these certainly make good sense in theory. Higher education struggles undoubtedly to adapt to digital technologies that are designed for other contexts and then 'imported' into university settings. This incongruity is perhaps most apparent with regards to the 'Office' applications that dominant many areas of university work. As should be apparent to anyone that has used it, for example, the PowerPoint presentation application was clearly developed for boardrooms and sales pitches rather than classroom learning. This raises the logical question of what a presentation application might look like if designed specifically for a university teaching and learning context. The same goes for word-processing applications such as Word. It is difficult to make a convincing pedagogic case for having 200 variations of typographic font (including Comic Sans and Wingdings) but only limited and rigid options for checking spelling, vocabulary and grammar. In the face of such constrained digital offerings, it seems reasonable to argue that universities – and the people that work within them – should be looking to engineer more appropriate alternatives.

This suggestion of encouraging the development of a 'people's technology' within universities is not as far-fetched as it might appear. The technological expertise and will to innovate that is required to instigate such change certainly can be found within higher education. As was acknowledged back in the preface to this book, the early computers and discipline of computer science were developed largely within university laboratories. Indeed, most of the substantial subsequent advancements in computing have had some origins in university-based research and development. Academics and universities are hardly the disempowered, low-skilled, excluded 'end users' that critical commentators are usually keen to get involved in the 'participatory design' and 'co-creation' of digital technology. On the contrary, most universities have a great deal of untapped in-house expertise regarding technology design, instructional design, human–computer interaction and so on. As such, it is not overly ambitious to imagine members of the academy seizing the initiative from multinational IT corporations and commercial developers, and building digital technologies that better suit their own circumstances and needs.

In light of all that has been discussed during the past seven chapters, this is clearly a conclusion worth considering. Yet we should be in no doubt over the practical difficulty of realizing this deceptively simple suggestion – not least in terms of the likely 'capture' and distortion of any successful alternate technology by the dominant interests and influences that it might be seeking to usurp. Any successful 'people's computer' or organically developed software application is likely to soon face the shaping forces and structures that have pervaded this book. Before setting off down this route, it is therefore important to recognize that building our way out of the problem of digital higher education may not be enough to permanently upset the status quo.

A pertinent example of this can be found in the development of MOOCs throughout the 2000s and 2010s. Mention of MOOCs has recurred throughout this book, often with regards to the emergence of large-scale programmes such as Coursera and edX over the first half of the 2010s. These are quasi-corporate ventures concerned with delivering university courses on a free-at-the-point-of-contact basis to mass audiences. Yet while some MOOCs are now multi-billion dollar businesses supporting many of the most prestigious global university 'brands', the concept was developed originally by a small group of radically minded university teachers and researchers. Specifically, the initial notion of the MOOC can be traced back to a loose collective of educational technologists in Canada, with a shared interest in developing open courses in online environments. This led to the idea of individuals being encouraged to learn through their own choice of digital tools – what was termed their 'personal learning networks' – the collective results of which could be aggregated by the course coordinators and shared with other students. Early efforts out of the Universities of Prince Edward Island, Manitoba and Athabasca focused on niche topics such as 'Connectivism and Connective Knowledge' and attracted a few thousand students each. In this original form, then, the MOOC was a grass-roots, counter-cultural attempt by technology-savvy educators to subvert the dominance of top-down models of traditional higher education provision. In its original state, the MOOC marked an audacious attempt to disrupt the problematic elements of institutionalized higher education, such as assessment, payment and an emphasis on mass instruction rather than individually directed discovery learning. In contrast to the commercially led MOOCs of today, this was not a model of learning designed to reap dividends for shareholders or reinforce the brand identity of the world's major-league universities.

That the radically minded MOOC model was swiftly adopted and adapted by individuals working within large higher education institutions such as Stanford, MIT and Harvard is perhaps understandable. That these efforts then led to well-financed and well-resourced initiatives such as edX and Coursera is also unsurprising given the correspondences between digital technology and commercial interests that have been highlighted throughout the course of this book. While trading on the MOOC banner and ethos, these concerns now involve the 'selling' of higher education hundreds of thousands of learners underpinned by complex revenue streams. As well as charging its partner universities around $250,000 for the online 'conversion' of each offline course, edX soon struck a deal with the education publisher Pearson to offer MOOC students the choice of paying to take proctored final examinations. Similarly, the Coursera business model evolved quickly to involve charging its millions of users for premium services, hosting paid-for advertising and the selling of student information to potential employers. In all these ways, the form, values and outcomes of what are now called 'MOOCs' are far removed from the initial intentions of the grass-roots originators. Indeed, some educational technologists have attempted vainly to sustain the original spirit of what they now distinguish as 'c-MOOCs' ('c' for connectivist) as opposed to the corporatized 'x-MOOCs'. Yet the financial might of elite institutions such as Harvard, Oxford and Melbourne has clearly prevailed, leaving the MOOC no longer an alternative to the mainstream business of higher education. In fact, there is every sign that the for-profit MOOC model could well become a template for the bulk of 'university' education in the future. Effectively challenging the long-term power structures and dominant interests of modern higher education is clearly not an easy task.

Looking for alternative solutions: working around the edges of higher education and technology

The 'corporate capture' and cannibalization of MOOCs by elite universities and business interests illustrates the complexity of any grass-roots attempt – however well intentioned and technologically capable – to 'build' alternative technologies for higher education. This is not to argue that further attempts along these lines should not continue, yet we need to be realistic of the chances of success. So what other options are there? Here it is useful to recall the point made at the beginning of the book that digital technology needs to be understood in a social as well as a technical sense. Indeed, much of what has been highlighted over the past seven chapters are not technical problems with possible technical solutions. Instead these problems are fundamentally social, political, economic and cultural in nature (e.g. the entrenched forms of commodification, exploitation and performativity that pervade universities). As such, the most appropriate ways of tackling these problems are likely to be social, political, economic and cultural in nature. In this sense, the answers to the problems outlined in this book are not likely to simply take the form of 'more technology', 'different technology' or 'new technology'. Instead, we need to ask what social, cultural, economic and political changes are possible and (most importantly) preferable.

So what forms might these attempts at 'social engineering' the conditions of digital higher education take? First, it is necessary to acknowledge that any changes will need to be many in number but also modest in their individual intent. As has already been established, the dominant interests and forces implicit in the current shaping of digital higher education are entrenched within deep-rooted power hierarchies and with the weight of history on their side. These are powerful interests that will not be disrupted or deterred easily. Rather than attempting to force immediate wholesale 'change', it makes more sense to think along reduced but more realistic lines – akin to the recent trend in public policy circles to think of 'nudges' and 'tweaks'. Rather than trying to re-engineer higher education on a grand scale, it might perhaps be more productive to adopt a small-scale, decentralized 'guerrilla' approach. These changes would involve the incremental social (re)engineering of different aspects of digital higher education. This is, of course, not the first time such an approach has been recommended. Indeed, these suggestions deliberately echo Michel de Certeau's (1984) notion of 'street-level tactics of resistance', and even Karl Popper's (1957/2002) assertion that change might be best achieved through 'piecemeal' adjustments and 'tinkering' rather than wholesale reform and revolution.

Looking back over the past seven chapters, there would appear to be plenty of possible opportunities to 'tweak' digital higher education in ways that might contribute to the eventual establishment of more equitable and less oppressive outcomes. In the brief space remaining, we shall confine ourselves to a handful of possible areas for change. All these suggestions centre on problematizing the digitization of higher education – making the issues highlighted so far in the book the focus of public controversy and the subject of sustained public dialogue and democratic reformation. Furthermore, many of these suggestions are also aimed at a subtle 'loosening-up' of digital arrangements within universities – making digital technology use less of an imposed 'top-down' process. So what *can* be done along these looser and more controversial lines? Let us revisit the socio-technical implications of the past seven chapters and consider the following possibilities.

Minding our language?

While it might appear a minor matter, an initial issue that merits serious consideration is that of challenging the language deployed to describe digital technology use in higher education. As philosophers from Wittgenstein to Foucault have pointed out, language is an integral element of the politics of everyday life – maintaining the parameters of what is, and what is not, seen as preferable and possible. Tweaking something as apparently trivial as the ways in which digital technology is talked about in higher education could well be a surprisingly effective means of altering the conditions of digital higher education. Language should therefore be recognized as a key part of shaping ideas and actions within educational contexts. As Gert Biesta (2005, p.54) reasons: 'language matters to education, because the language or languages we have available to speak about education determine to a large extent what can be said and done, and thus what cannot be said and done'.

As we have seen throughout this book, the words, phrases and terms used within higher education to describe digital processes and practices are highly charged and value-laden – conveying a definite sense of what should be happening, and often silencing other possibilities. For example, as Jones (2013) notes, the term 'learning technology' builds in a clear human purpose for the technology – which is positioned as tool that is to be deployed in the pursuit of learning. As such, the labels attached to technology practices and processes within higher education 'are intertwined with particular social practices and ethnical and political choices' (Jones 2013, p.163).

Indeed, the language of educational technology has developed distinct lexical, grammatical and stylistic characteristics of its very own – particularly in recent years as more and more groups and interests have become concerned with claiming a stake in determining what is 'educational technology'. This language of educational technology (what could be termed 'ed-tech speak') has shifted over the past twenty years from relatively straightforward descriptions of function and form to more subtle declarations of desired outcome. This linguistic transition has occurred in at least three ways. First is the increased use of active, deterministic descriptions of the core relationships between technology and education – predominantly based around what Gert Biesta (2005) identifies as 'the language of learning'. Here the role of education is to 'meet the needs of the learner' at whatever cost. Second is a heightened language of effect – often in evocative terms of 'impact' or 'transformation', where technology is presumed to be assisting or causing change to occur. Third is an increasingly emotive and often personalized register, involving the use of language that is variously playful, homespun and self-consciously appealing (take, for example, the notions of 'digital sandpits', 'digital dojos', computers called 'Raspberry Pi' and so on).

The restrictive effect of these linguistic turns can be seen throughout the past seven chapters – albeit in often subtle ways. Take, for example, the shifting ways that the entire field of educational technology has been described and self-styled over the past few decades. From the 1980s, a distinct shift occurred from 'computer-based instruction' to 'computer-assisted learning', and then later in the 2000s to 'technology-enhanced learning'. Underpinning these changes in language is an inference that learning is not only taking place, but that it is also being driven actively by the use of technology. To talk of 'technology-enhanced learning' or 'computer-supported collaborative learning' therefore has deliberate connotations. These politics of language are also evident in the slippery nature of the words and phrases that have come to describe digital products and processes at large within contemporary higher education. For example, people now talk far less about 'learning management systems' and far more about 'virtual learning environments' when referring to software platforms such as Moodle, Blackboard and so on. The semantic differences between the top-down, regulatory notion of a 'learning management system' and the active, free-form implications of a 'virtual learning environment' are considerable. Who would want to have their learning managed by a system when they could be immersed virtually in an environment of learning? The seductive and manipulative nature of such language is clear, but easy to become inured to.

As with all the best linguistic sleights of hand (see, for example, the language of advertising, political rhetoric or legalese), these recent forms of 'ed-tech speak' certainly do not reflect the whole picture of digital technology use in higher education. In this sense, one of the key elements in the fight against the injustices, inequalities and impositions of digital higher education could be the promotion of an alternate language for educational technology – a counter-lexicon that reflects more accurately the conflicts, compromises and exclusions that are at play. One possibility would be to support a reversion back to more objective descriptions. Why not refer to Moodle, Blackboard and similar applications as 'teaching management systems' or 'instruction management systems'? Why not acknowledge that online spaces designed to elicit forms of student contribution are not 'hangouts' or 'cafés', but places for 'required response' or 'mandatory comment'? Why not refer to online 'work groups' rather than 'learning communities'? Why not acknowledge that students are 'co-operating' rather than 'collaborating'?

A more radical alternative would be to broker explicitly 'honest' declarations of the likely consequences of digital technology use. Perhaps we need a language of higher education and technology that more accurately describes the underlying functions of these technologies and exposes their political intent. Thinking back to the issues that have emerged throughout this book, how might practices of monitoring, measurement, comparison, surveillance and performativity be better reflected in the language used to describe these technologies? Could we foster talk of 'digital resource dumps', 'content delivery services' or 'teacher monitoring systems' within higher education? The increased use of terms and phrases such as this would certainly help to forge a common sense amongst those to whom digital technology is 'done to' within universities – 'building identity, fostering an awareness of commonality and a basis for solidarity or *fraternité*' (Standing 2011, p.3).

Rescripting spaces, places and materialities

As well as thinking 'otherwise' about the language that is being deployed, we could also think differently about the spaces and places of digital education. As was acknowledged in Chapter 6, it is all too easy when discussing the digital aspects of higher education to look past the built environment and physical places of the contemporary university. Whether newly built or centuries old, most campuses are home to an awkward assortment of ugly-looking obstacles that constrain action and usually have to be 'worked around' rather than 'worked with'. A strong case can therefore be made for giving serious thought towards reconfiguring universities as 'quality public spaces' (Standing 2011, p.129). By this we are not referring to places designed primarily to log-in, tweet or text from. Rather we are seeking to develop quality spaces in which to physically move and interact with others on a face-to-face basis. The present trend to redesign and realign universities as places most suited to accessing and using digital technology (and thereby switching off from one's immediate surroundings) could be seen to be a worrying trend. As Standing (2011, p.129) concludes, 'a sense of territoriality is a human trait that is part of our genes. Cramp it and empty it of developmental meaning, and the result will be ugly.' As such, we need to design spaces of higher education that promote a higher quality but lower quantity of technology use.

One of the key ways in which the physical and material aspects of the university could be rethought is to better draw attention to the technologies that are being used within them. In this sense, the built environment can be reconfigured and redesigned in overtly political ways that draw attention to – and provoke reflection on – the nature of our digital technology use. As Lisa Parks (2009, n.p.) reasons, it is everyone's duty as infrastructural 'citizen/users' to be aware of the 'systems that surround [us] and that [we] subsidize and use'. Park suggests that new ways could be devised of 'visualizing and developing literacy about infrastructures and the relations that take shape through and around them'. Thus the digital technologies that shape the experience of working, studying and living in a university can be foregrounded and problematized, encouraging all workers and students to engage in conversations about access, usage and ownership. As Parks continues:

> While concealing infrastructure sites may be a viable aspect of urban planning (as has long been the case of sewer, electricity and water systems), one of its effects is to keep citizen/users naive about the systems that surround them and that they subsidize and use. Because of this, it is important to devise other ways of visualizing and developing literacy about infrastructures and the relations that take shape through and around them. Are there ways of representing [digital infrastructures] that will encourage citizens to participate in sustained discussions and decisions about network ownership, development, and access? What is it about infrastructure that is aesthetically unappealing? What form should infrastructure sites assume? Should they be visible or invisible?

Shannon Mattern (2012) offers a number of suggestions as to what forms this 'literacy' about digital infrastructure might take. For example, she proposes drawing attention to the politics of technology use by aestheticizing the wires, pipe, tubes, ducts and other physical conduits that constitute the physical infrastructure of digital technology use. Much like the trend for 1990s' 'raw' domestic architecture, university buildings could be stripped back to expose the fixtures and fittings of the digital age. Why not relocate cabling on the outside of walls, thereby making an aesthetic and political 'feature' of what is usually hidden away from sight and mind? In terms of drawing attention to the environmental politics of technology use, Mattern raises the possibility of visualizing broadband usage or amplifying the hum of electrical currents. Why not alter the level of lighting on individuals depending on the amount of bandwidth that they are using? All these ideas (however far-fetched) at least provoke us to think more carefully about the possibilities of designing spaces and places that make people aware of the infrastructures (and their attendant politics) that deliver their 'free' information.

Conversely, more thought could also be given to de-scripting or even re-scripting the digital construction of spaces within the contemporary university setting. How can the prescribed intentions and agendas of buildings, rooms and other public spaces be subverted and made more open and 'writerly' in nature (Andersen and Pold 2011)? How can the built environment be used as a means of reprogramming people's uses of digital technology (rather than allowing digital technology to reprogram people's use of space)? For example, there are a number of possible ways that the built environment of a university might be 'rewritten' or 'hacked' to reshape digital technology use. Notwithstanding the legality of such practices, mobile phone 'jammers' and wireless 'blocking' devices have been used in some cinemas, churches, prisons and concert venues, and are now available in portable forms that could be brought in and out of teaching and meeting spaces as appropriate. Alternatively, inspiration could be taken from the amateur 'building hackers' who interface with 'building management systems' and IT infrastructures to turn technology usage data into publically visible displays that are meaningful to the people working in those buildings. In this sense, building-related data are accessed unofficially, displayed in a way that highlights the political nature of what is represents, and are therefore made the subject of public conversation.

Collective ways of supporting a smarter use of digital technology

These suggestions for the 'rebuilding' of the material and linguistic manifestations of digital technology use bring us on to the broader point of shifting the cultures of digital education along 'smarter' lines. By 'smarter' we are implying values of fairness, respect, social justice, humanity, ethically and publicly minded conduct. As with the rescripting of space and place just described, how might it be possible to set about rescripting digital technology use within higher education with more socially concerned, equitable values? Of course, altering cultural understandings and values is not a straightforward process, and any individual effort may well appear too slight and marginal to make any meaningful difference on its own. Yet it is important to recognize that cultural change is a gradual and incremental process. If enough separate attempts are made to draw attention to the injustices, inequalities and inefficiencies of current digital technology use within higher education, then shifts in people's thinking, expectations and actions might occur.

One possibility is for concerned members of higher education communities to actively and publically voice their collective concerns. Already this has happened in response to the rapid growth of commercially provided online learning over the past five years. In the last few months of 2012, for example, a group of concerned and 'passionate' academics, tutors, CEOs and journalists convened in the heart of Silicon Valley, collaboratively producing an ambitiously titled 'Bill of Rights and Principles for Learning in the Digital Age'. This group contained some of the great and good from the US educational technology community, including long-time 'open education' advocate John Seely Brown and Sebastian Thrun (the previously mentioned Stanford University Professor in Computer Science whose open course on artificial intelligence led to his founding of Udacity Inc. and the mainstream emergence of commercial MOOCs). While leaving themselves open to criticism by not including any full-time 'learners' in their ranks, this group's efforts provoked a considerable reaction within higher education circles. As an exercise in collective reflection and collective responsibility on the part of the higher education 'ed-tech' community, the Palo Alto 'Bill of Rights' offers a good example of thinking otherwise about the values of digital higher education.

Some of the Bill's declarations are straightforward enough. In terms of access, for example, it reasonably states that online learning 'should be affordable and available [to all]'. Yet the document also evokes a number of discussions that are less often acknowledged in higher education circles, such as privacy, intellectual property, non-exploitation of teaching staff, financial transparency and the detrimental effects of commodification. The Bill also highlights a set of alternative learning outcomes involving qualities such as curiosity, passion, imagination and wonder. For example, as is stated at various points:

- 'Student privacy is an inalienable right . . . Students have a right to know how data collected about their participation in the online system will be used by the organization and made available to others.
- Students also have the right to create and own intellectual property and data associated with their participation in online courses.
- Students have a right to know how their participation supports the financial health of the online system in which they are participating.
- Students have the right to care, diligence, commitment, honesty and innovation. They are not being sold a product – nor are they the product being sold. They are not just consumers. Education is also about trust. Learning – not corporate profit – is the principal purpose of all education.
- The right to have great teachers . . . students should expect – indeed demand – that the people arranging, mentoring and facilitating their learning online be financially, intellectually and pedagogically valued and supported by institutions of higher learning and by society.
- Open online education should inspire the unexpected, experimentation, and questioning – in other words, encourage play. We must cultivate the imagination and the dispositions of questing, tinkering and connecting. We must remember that the best learning, above all, imparts the gift of curiosity, the wonder of accomplishment, and the passion to know and learn even more.'

These principles certainly challenge many of the worst excesses of the 'massification' on online learning within universities over the past few years, and draw attention eloquently to a number of critical issues associated with the growing commercial market for online higher education. Similar sentiments can be found in the earlier 'Manifesto for teaching online' first produced by teachers and researchers from the University of Edinburgh in 2010. Here another provocative yet thoughtful set of principles was proposed, including at various points the notions that:

- 'Every course design is philosophy and belief in action;
- Online teaching should not be downgraded into "facilitation";
- The aesthetics of online course design are too readily neglected: courses that are fair of (inter)face are better places to teach and learn in;
- Online courses are prone to cultures of surveillance: our visibility to each other is a pedagogical and ethical issue;
- Assessment strategies can be designed to allow for the possibility of resistance;
- A routine of plagiarism detection structures is a relation of distrust;
- Assessment is a creative crisis as much as it is a statement of knowledge.'

Public statements such as these act to direct attention towards values and concerns that have tended to be sidelined – if not silenced – in the mainstream rush towards the digitization of higher education. One certainly does not often hear talk of respect, care, diligence, aesthetics, good design and enjoyment when it comes to e-learning. The long-term influence of these public pronouncements remains to be seen, but in the short term they offer valuable rejoinders to the dominant discourses that so quickly can engulf and define developments in digital education. Could it make sense for concerned educators in every country to follow suit? Could similar manifestos and bills of rights be produced for campus-based and 'blended learning'? How might similar manifestos be formulated for the technology-based work of university professional and academic staff? Certainly, the clear and forceful collective expression of alternate values and principles needs to be explored.

Individual ways of supporting a smarter use of digital technology

Of course, there are limits to the number of times that grand declarations of intent can be made effectively by representatives of the higher education and technology 'communities'. We also need to consider how the 're-valuing' of digital education might take place at everyday levels of individual action and resistance. In this sense, there is perhaps a need for localized groups of individuals to engage in forms of sustained dialogue about the digital technologies that they are using, the ways in which they are using them and the ways in which they would like to be using them. More important still is the question of how alternate values might be inscribed into the digital products, processes and practices on campus.

There are a number of examples of individual, localized action that might provide inspiration. For instance, in 2011 an Austrian law student – Max Schrems –

exercised his 'right to access' under European law everything that Facebook knew about him. While Facebook initially resisted this imposition, eventually they were forced to provide Mr Schrems with a file over 1,200 pages long. This included his entire history of 'friending' and 'de-friending', his responses to invitations, records of other people who has signed onto Facebook on the same computers as him, email addresses that he had not provided to Facebook but that had been retrieved from his 'friends' contact books, and a large number of messages and online conversations that Mr Schrems had long since deleted from Facebook (the company helpfully added the notation 'deleted' to these particular records). In order to counter similar challenges, Facebook subsequently added features that allow users (if they look hard enough) to access some of the personal data that the company has stored on them. These actions of one master's degree student in the face of one of the world's largest and most powerful corporations should therefore give hope to any 'end user'. Why could this victory (of sorts) not be repeated in university contexts? Why should any individual – teacher, student, administrator – not be able to see all the data held on them in the university's systems as a matter of course? Why should university authorities or external providers of university digital services not be held to account for their digital actions in a similar manner to a company such as Facebook?

Indeed, there is no reason why groups within higher education should not oppose any manner of alternate arrangements with regards to the ways that digital technologies are used in their name. Take, for example, two of the more invidious applications and services that have recurred throughout this book – the (mis)use of email and PowerPoint. In an effort to counter the 'abuse' of email communication, many universities have developed tokenistic guidelines for 'email etiquette' and 'acceptable use' that tend to focus on issues of respect, courtesy and so on. Such notions of 'acceptable' use could be extended, however, to counter the shaping of email communication along overly bureaucratic and managerial lines – not least to curtail the high volume, 'always-on' nature of online communication within universities. Why not set limits to number of emails that an individual can send each day? Why not limit the times that email can be accessed within office working hours, or at the beginning of each day? Why not disable the pernicious practices of 'cc-ing' and 'bcc-ing'?

Similarly, in terms of the use of PowerPoint as a teaching resource, why not restrict slides only to information that is *not* provided in another form (i.e. as a spoken element of a lecture or in a hand-out)? Why not restrict slides to only pictoral or graphical content (i.e. containing no text at all)? This might well put an end to lectures that consist of teachers reading a list of bullet points for an hour. Similarly, in terms of on-campus and off-campus working practices, why not encourage a default expectation of an individual always being offline rather than online? Why not deny staff the ability to access university systems from their homes, or at weekends? These suggestions might appear trivial, unworkable or flippant – yet they highlight the more serious point that the use of digital technology within our universities does not have to be the way that it is. It *is* possible to change some of the worst excesses fairly simply, providing that there is first a collective recognition of the problematic nature of such digital practices, and then a collective will to make changes for the better.

Expanding the publics of digital higher education

These examples all point to the fact that many of the problems of contemporary digital higher education can be challenged through increased dialogue. Indeed, much of what has been argued for in this chapter so far relates to establishing digital technology use in higher education as a democratic process. In this sense, a crucial step is establishing digital higher education as a contested public space – i.e. as a topic that requires open discussion, open argument and critical scrutiny. The tactic here, then, would not be to ignore the vested interests and agendas that dominate the current shaping of digital higher education, but to contest them through open argument. If the contradictions, deficiencies and flawed rhetoric of the past forty years of digital technology use in higher education could be exposed publically, then there might be greater chance for the interests of the currently 'under-served' majority to hold sway over the interests of the 'super-served' elite. These debates should publicize, politicize and problematize the forms of technology described in this book, in a manner that provokes a mass interest in digital higher education as a public issue.

Of course, public engagement with any issue cannot be imposed but must be encouraged and nurtured through publicity. This itself is not an easy task, especially given the long-standing impoverished condition of recent public discourse and debate with regards to digital technology and higher education. This is not a problem that is particular to higher education. One of the frustrating features of popular public understandings of digital technology is the almost subconscious framing of 'digital technology' as a topic that people are conditioned to not think deeply about. This occurs either because of an assumed lack of access to 'expert' knowledge, perceptions of the inevitable direction of technological development and 'progress', or simply because of the sheer ubiquity of digital technology use throughout everyday life. At best, non-expert 'lay' users are flattered into thinking that digital technology gives them enhanced agency and control to the extent that there is little need to question the wider arrangements of digital society beyond one's immediate personal experience. As such, public awareness of technology use in educational settings has long been shaped disproportionately by elite interests (such as professional technologists, the IT industry and other corporate actors).

One of the first steps to wider public dialogue is debunking the notion of technological expertise within educational circles. As Brian Wynne (1996) reasons, one does not need to know how a nuclear power plant operates in order to have a thoughtful and well-considered opinion on how they should be used in one's community. This implies the sustained inclusion of *all* interests and stakeholders in the circuits of debate and influence that surround digital technology use in higher education. Above all, this would involve the increased inclusion of 'ordinary' but often marginalized users and non-users of digital higher educa-tion – i.e. students, graduate employers, adjunct and other short-term contracted teachers and other 'groups of concerned citizens and the general public which may be both excited by and feel powerless in the face of scientific advance' (Mat-thewman 2011, p.120). From this perspective, all people in and around higher education should be seen as having valid views and concerns – from the most dis-engaged student to the most marginalized academic or over-worked administra-tor. Regardless of their personal passion (or lack of passion) for technology, these are all key components of establishing digital higher education as a democratic process. These are voices that need to be given equal status to those of university authorities, e-learning consultants and IT industry interests.

Once these conditions can be established, then there is a range of existing public and participatory techniques that can be taken advantage of. These include citizen's juries, expert panels, public hearings, consensus conferences and delib-eration polling – all of which have been used with some success in increasing public participation in areas such as environmental and health policy. In all these cases, it is important that these extended higher education publics are involved in a manner that moves beyond tokenistic processes of being 'consulted', 'informed' as to what is 'best' for them, or positioned in a reduced role of expressing 'learner voice' or 'consumer voice'. Instead, the aim would be to openly discuss and facili-tate the meaningful re-arrangement of digital technology use within the univer-sity sector. These conversations would seek to challenge the legitimacy of current dominant understandings, develop long-term views on how digital technologies should and should not be embedded in work and organizational practices, and to collectively consider and promote a 'good sense' rather than a 'common-sense' about higher education and digital technology.

Involving more actors in the politics of digital technology and higher education

Of course, care needs to be taken not to place an excessive burden on these popu-lar participatory processes. Public engagement and the development of coun-ter-arguments and alternate arrangements are important, yet will only be fully effective alongside more substantial changes to the governance and regulation of the application of digital technology in higher education. Thus as well as sup-porting these mass forms of public engagement, attention also needs to be paid to the agendas and actions of some of the large organizations that might have a capacity to influence the nature and form of how digital technologies are used within universities. Indeed, it could be argued that many of the publics identified above would require a considerable amount of support in discovering a collective, critical voice. Left to their own devices, there is little sense that change would necessarily emerge naturally from any of these groups. For example, as Brendan Cantwell (2013) observes somewhat fatalistically, faculty activism may be an obvi-ous challenge to the undesirable recent changes in higher education, but this could be seen 'to be as likely as the prospects for a global agreement on climate change'. Thus as Langdon Winner (1998, p.377) concurs, the critical changes that have been recommended in this book would certainly require the stimulation of a hitherto dormant desire for activism and organized opposition: 'the goal of shaping information technology to democratize education is highly appealing, but there are, at present, no strong, well-organized forces promoting that end'.

In this sense, it might be possible to mobilize the interests and actions of organizations that traditionally have offered defence against other forms of dominance and injustice. These organizations might include trade unions, community groups and other areas of civil society such as non-government organizations, voluntary groups and charities. Teaching and lecturing unions, for example, could engage more actively with the worst excesses of digital exploitation – treating the introduction of a new learning system or digital infrastructure as a controversial action that requires scrutiny, consultation and possible opposition. In short, all aspects of digital education should be seen as a 'union matter' in the same way as a new employment or pension procedure. Similarly, student unions could engage more proactively with the development and introduction of digital processes and practices within universities – insisting on their right to contribute a collective and politically engaged input into any procurement of systems or development of infrastructures that will impact on students. In short, student unions need to make digital technology an integral part of campus politics – recognizing university technology systems as sites of struggle where students' needs and demands should be better represented. There is perhaps also room here for unions to form alliances with technically adept and radically minded oppositional groups that make use of digital media, such as 'indy media', hackivist and other alternative technology movements. The aim here would be to encourage the closer involvement and interactions between mass publics of higher education and mass publics of digital media that have otherwise been too disaggregated and remote to establish sustained connections.

Thinking along these expanded lines, how might the state be involved more directly in the changing nature of digital higher education? At present state involvement in technology use in any sector of education has tended to be limited. Obviously states have limited purchase on the actions of universities, and only a limited capacity in developing and producing digital technologies. As recent history in countries such as the UK has shown, large-scale, government-run IT programmes are often unwieldy, over-expensive and vastly inefficient. As such, states have tended to restrict themselves to creating 'good climates' for the digitization of education provision to take place, and acting as cheerleaders for the broad adoption of digital technology throughout all areas of the public sector. In general, state actors have played minimal roles in actively shaping or directing the values and nature of technology use in education – especially in the relatively autonomous higher education sector.

Yet, in the face of everything that has been discussed throughout this book, the state is perhaps one of the only institutions capable of directing, regulating and controlling the use of digital technology within public education along socially 'fairer' lines. This need not involve a dirigiste arrangement of state-controlled technology. Instead digital higher education could be subject to a greater amount of what Archon Fung and Erik Wright (2003) term 'empowered participatory governance' – i.e. where government and state agencies are charged with being more responsible and more responsive to the conditions of digital education. In this sense there are a number of areas in which responsible states might be involved in the governance and regulation of educational technology. For instance, the state has a potential role to play in the regulation of the marketplace for online education provision – even at the level of restricting what can be considered as an online 'degree' or 'university'. Aside from assuming a more central role in directing technological development, state actors might also play a part in regulating technology use within university systems. Given that in many countries the state retains a regulatory role in higher education, why should digital higher education not be a focus for increased state scrutiny? This might involve ensuring that university authorities display a sustained commitment to maintaining, protecting and improving physical 'bricks and mortar' institutions of the university, rather than allowing digital technology to be seen as offering a viable alternative. If functioning along democratic, publically minded lines, then the state is perhaps one of the few organizations capable of providing an effective check and balance against the increasingly 'business-orientated' concerns of other higher education interests.

Alternatively, there may also be scope for states to more forcibly direct – if not control – forms of commercial activity in digital higher education as part of regulating companies' commitments to 'corporate social responsibility'. Thus, rather than allowing multinational IT corporations carte blanche to profiteer from the digitization of public universities, states might seek to restrict and regulate the educational activities of these companies – perhaps as recompense for being to operate freely within other areas of society. Indeed, the IT industry could be forced to engage with higher education markets on a pro bono rather than purely for-profit basis – acknowledging the wider societal benefit of supporting the use of digital technology within universities. Additionally, IT producers could be required to work more closely with higher education 'end users' in designing and developing genuinely appropriate technology devices and application for the university context. This could involve the development of alternative architectures and formats of digital technology that better fit the needs and purposes of public higher education. Encouraging the genuine involvement of educational actors in the development process could, therefore, be of benefit to everyone involved.

Conclusions

On one hand, these might appear to be wildly utopian and largely impractical suggestions for change. Yet such conclusions are no more utopian and impractical than the usual techno-centric 'boosterism' that has sustained the field of educational technology for the past forty years or so. If we are to take seriously

Gramsci's notion of retaining an 'optimism because of will' alongside a 'pessimism because of intelligence', then it is necessary to counter the digital hype that pervades higher education with more socially focused and publically minded concerns – however high-minded they might appear. As such, all of the ideas just put forward in this chapter are not 'solutions' that can be immediately implemented in order to somehow 'solve' the deep-rooted problems that clearly beset contemporary higher education. Rather these are intended to be starting points for the very difficult conversations that need to take place about what digital higher education is, and what digital higher education should be. At this late stage in the book, it is important to recognize that there are no neat solutions – only the need to continue acknowledging and exploring the critical questions and issues that clearly underpin the ongoing digitalization of higher education.

As such, the 'take home message' of this book (for readers who look for that sort of thing) is that digital technology is a site of complex struggle for control of the heart and spirit of the public university system. Digital technology is not a solution to any of the problems that currently beset universities – in fact digital technology is more accurately understood as a set of problems posing as solutions. We therefore need an academic community that is willing and able to ask these questions and investigate these issues. We need a new breed of academic researchers who are not content to simply explore the 'state-of-the-art' of new technology developments, but ready to roll up their sleeves and grapple with the disappointing realities of digital education – what could be termed the 'state-of-the-actual'. Most importantly, we need a higher education community that is able to take time to talk seriously about these issues – that is prepared to make the digital technology in higher education a site of 'extraordinary conversation' and dialogue. It should be possible for everyone in higher education to insist on different digital futures than are currently set in place.

Hopefully this book has provided a starting point for such conversations. As such, it is best to treat this book as a question rather than an answer – as John Holloway (2002, p.215) puts it, 'an invitation to discuss'. Feel free to disagree with everything that has been argued over the past eight chapters, but then ask yourself *why* you disagree . . . and then ask yourself what *you* think should be done instead. Most importantly of all, share your thoughts with others – not only in the self-congratulatory and self-confirmatory 'bubble' of Twitter and the blogosphere, but in the corridors, common rooms and coffee shops of the universities that you work in. There is an urgent need to establish the use of digital technology in higher education as a site of genuine controversy and resistance, rather than an unthinking consensus. The fight back starts here.

References

3M (2007) *Create a more human library: RFID 101.* St Paul MN, 3M Library Systems.

Aleman, A. and Wartman, K. (2009) *Online social networking on campus: understanding what matters in student culture.* New York, Routledge.

Allen-Collinson, J. (2007) 'Get yourself some nice, neat, matching box files: research administrators and occupational identity work'. *Studies in Higher Education,* 32, 3, pp.295–309.

Anderson, C. (2009) *Free: the future of a radical price.* New York, Hyperion.

Andersen, C. and Pold, S. (2011) 'The scripted spaces of urban ubiquitous computing: the experience, poetics and politics of public scripted space'. *Fibreculture,* 19, FCJ-133, http://fibreculturejournal.org/wp-content/pdfs/FCJ-133Andersen%20Pold.pdf.

Appadurai, A. (2005) 'Commodities and the politics of value', in Ertman, M. and Williams, J. (eds) *Rethinking commodification.* New York, New York University Press (pp.34–45).

Apperley, T. (2009) *Gaming rhythms: play and counterplay from the situated to the global.* Amsterdam, Institute of Network Cultures.

Apple, M. (2010a) 'The measure of success', in Monahan, T. and Torres, R. (eds) *Schools under surveillance.* New Brunswick NJ, Rutgers University Press (pp.175–192).

Apple, M. (2010b) *Global crises, social justice, and education.* London, Routledge.

Apple, M., Ball, S. and Gandin, L. (2010) 'Mapping the sociology of education: social context, power and knowledge', in Apple, M., Ball, S. and Gandin, L. (eds) *The Routledge international handbook of the sociology of education.* New York, Routledge (pp.1–12).

Ashworth, P., Bannister, P. and Thorne, P. (1997) 'Guilty in whose eyes? University students' perceptions of cheating and plagiarism in academic work and assessment'. *Studies in Higher Education,* 22, 2, pp.187–203.

Aspromourgos, A. (2012) 'The managerialist university: an economic interpretation'. *Australian Universities' Review,* 54, 2, pp.44–49.

Augé, M. (1995) [trans. Howe, J.] *Non-places: introduction to an anthropology of supermodernity.* London, Verso.

Bailey, M. and Freedman, D. (2012) *The assault on universities: a manifesto for resistance.* London, Pluto.

Ball, S. (2012) *Global education Inc: new policy networks and neoliberal imaginary.* London, Routledge.

Barber, M., Donnelly, K. and Rizvi, S. (2013) *An avalanche is coming: higher education and the revolution ahead.* London, Institute for Public Policy Research.

Barley, S. and Kunda, G. (2001) 'Bringing work back in'. *Organization Science*, 12, pp.76–95.

Barnard, S., Hassan, T., Dainty, A. and Bagilhole, B. (2013) 'Interdisciplinary content, contestations of knowledge and informational transparency in engineering curriculum'. *Teaching in Higher Education*, 18, 7, pp.748–760.

Barnett, R. (2011) *Being a university*. London, Routledge.

Barrett, P., Zhang, Y., Moffat, J. and Kobbacy, K. (2013) 'An holistic, multi-level analysis identifying the impact of classroom design on pupils' learning'. *Building and Environment*, 59, pp.678–689.

Barrow, M. (2006) 'Assessment and student transformation: linking character and intellect'. *Studies in Higher Education*, 31, 3, pp.357–372.

Bauman, Z. (2001) *The individualized society*. Cambridge, Polity.

Bauman, Z. (2005) *Liquid life*. Cambridge, Polity.

Bauman, Z. (2010) *Forty-four letters from the liquid modern world*. Cambridge, Polity.

Bauman, Z. and Lyon, D. (2013) *Liquid surveillance*. Cambridge, Polity.

Bebbington, W. (2012) 'Déjà vu all over again: what next for universities?' *Australian Universities' Review*, 54, 2, pp.73–77.

Becker, G. (1975) *Human capital: a theoretical and empirical analysis*. Chicago, University of Chicago Press.

Behenna, S. and Schulz, L. (2011) 'New ways of managing change in the workplace', in *Tertiary Education and Management Conference 2011 Refereed Papers* (pp.13–28).

Benson, L. and Harkavy, I. (2002) 'Saving the soul of the university: what is to be done?', in Robins, K. and Webster, F. (eds) *The virtual university: knowledge, markets and management*. Oxford, Oxford University Press (pp.169–209).

Biesta, G. (2005) 'Against learning: reclaiming a language for education in an age of learning'. *Nordisk Pedagogik*, 25, pp.54–66.

Bigum, C. and Kenway, J. (1998) 'New information technologies and the ambiguous future of schooling: some possible scenarios', in Hargreaves, A., Lieberman, A. and Fullan, M. (eds) *International handbook of educational change*. Berlin, Springer (pp.95–115).

Bijker, W. (2010) 'How is technology made? That is the question!' *Cambridge Journal of Economics*, 34, pp.63–76.

'Bill of Rights and Principles for Learning in the Digital Age' (2012) https://github.com/audreywatters/learnersrights/blob/master/bill_of_rights.md.

Blum, A. (2012) *Tubes: behind the scenes at the internet*. London, Penguin.

Boltanski, L. and Chiapello, E. (1999/2005) [trans. Elliott, G.] *The new spirit of capitalism*. London, Verso.

Bondarouk, T. and Ruël, H. (2009) 'Electronic human resource management: challenges in the digital era'. *The International Journal of Human Resource Management*, 20, 3, pp.505–514.

Boud, D. (1995) 'Assessment and learning?', in Knight, P. (ed.) *Assessment for learning in higher education*. London, Kogan Page (pp.35–48).

Bourdieu, P. and Passeron, J. (1977) *Reproduction in education, society and culture*. London, Sage.

Boyer, E. (1990) *Scholarship reconsidered: priorities of the professoriate*. Princeton NJ, Carnegie Foundation for the Advancement of Teaching.

Brabazon, T. (2002) *Digital hemlock: internet education and the poisoning of teaching*. Sydney, University of New South Wales Press.

Brabazon, T. (2007) *The university of Google*. Aldershot, Ashgate

Bradwell, P. (2009) *The edgeless university: why higher education must embrace technology.* London, Demos.

Brand, S. (1994) *How buildings learn: what happens after they're built.* London, Phoenix.

Braverman, H. (1974) *Labour and monopoly capital.* New York, Monthly Review Press.

Breen, L. and Maassen, M. (2005) 'Reducing the incidence of plagiarism in an undergraduate course: the role of education'. *Issues In Educational Research*, 15, www.iier.org.au/iier15/breen.html.

Brehony, K. (2002) 'Researching the "grammar of schooling": an historical view'. *European Educational Research Journal*, 1, 1, pp.178–189.

Breivik, P. (1998) *Student learning in the information age.* Phoenix, Oryz Press.

Brotcorne, P. (2005) 'Making sense of the internet: exploring students use of internet-based information resources in university', paper presented at the *British Educational Research Association Annual Conference*, University of Glamorgan, 14–17 September.

Brown, J. (2011) 'Salford University's digital campus: "This is not a place you come to read books"'. *The Independent*, 3 November.

Brown, P., Lauder, H. and Ashton, D. (2008) 'Education, globalisation and the future of the knowledge economy'. *European Educational Research Journal*, 7, 2, pp.131–156.

Brown, P., Lauder, H. and Ashton, D. (2011) *The global auction: the broken promises of education, jobs and incomes.* Oxford, Oxford University Press.

Bruns, A. (2008) *Blogs, Wikipedia, Second Life and beyond.* New York, Peter Lang.

Buckingham, D. (2011) 'Foreword', in Thomas, M. (ed.) *Deconstructing digital natives.* London, Routledge (pp.ix–xi).

Burawoy, M. (2011) 'On uncompromising pessimism: response to my critics'. *Global Labor Journal*, 2, 1, pp.73–77.

Calderon, A. (2012) 'Massification continues to transform higher education'. *University World News*, 2 September, 237, www.universityworldnews.com/article.php?story=20120831155341147.

Calhoun, C. (1992) 'The infrastructure of modernity: indirect social relationships, information technology, and social integration', in Haferkamp, H. and Smelser, N. (eds) *Social change and modernity.* Berkeley CA, University of California Press (pp.205–236).

Calhoun, C. (1998) 'Community without propinquity revisited: communications technology and the transformation of the urban public sphere'. *Sociological Inquiry*, 68, 3, pp.373–397.

Campanelli, V. (2010) *Web aesthetics: how digital media affect culture and society.* Amsterdam, NAi Publishers.

Cantwell, B. (2013) 'Assessing the public university'. *British Journal of Sociology of Education*, 34, 1, pp.152–161.

Case, J. (2013) *Researching student learning in higher education.* London, Routledge.

Castells, M. (1996) *The rise of the network society.* Oxford, Blackwell.

Castells, M. (2009) *Communication power.* Oxford, Oxford University Press.

Castronova, E. (2006) *Synthetic worlds: the business and culture of online games.* Chicago, Chicago University Press.

Chakravartty, P. and Sarikakis, K. (2006) *Media policy and globalization.* New York, Palgrave Macmillan.

Cheung, W. and Huang, W. (2005) 'Proposing a framework to assess internet usage in university education'. *British Journal of Educational Technology*, 36, 2, pp.237–253.

Christensen, J. and McCabe, D. (2006) 'Understanding academic misconduct'. *The Canadian Journal of Higher Education*, 36, 1, pp.49–63.

Clark, B. (1998) *Creating entrepreneurial universities*. New York, Elsevier.

Cooley, M. (1999) 'Human-centred design', in Jacobson, R. (ed.) *Information design*. Cambridge MA, MIT Press (pp.59–83).

Cooper, S. (2002) *Technoculture and critical theory: in the service of the machine*. London, Routledge.

Couldry, N. (2010) *Why voice matters: culture and politics and neoliberalism*. London, Routledge.

Crafti, S. (2012) 'RMIT's latest is a building to navigate as well as to inhabit'. *The Age*, 20 August.

Crook, C. (2008) 'Theories of formal and informal learning in the world of web 2.0', in Livingstone, S. (ed.) *Theorizing the benefits of new technology for youth*. Oxford, University of Oxford (pp.30–37).

Crouch, C. (2011) *The strange non-death of neoliberalism*. Cambridge, Polity.

Dale, R. (2005) 'Globalisation, knowledge economy and comparative education'. *Comparative Education*, 41, 2, pp.117–149.

Daniel, J. (2009) 'The expansion of higher education in the developing world', in Vrasidas, C., Zembylas, M. and Glass, G. (eds) *ICT for education, development and social justice*. Charlotte NC, Information Age (pp.53–63).

Daniel, Y. (2008) 'The textualised student', in DeVault, M. (ed.) *People at work*. New York, New York University Press (pp.248–265).

David, M. and Naidoo, R. (2013) *The sociology of higher education: reproduction, transformation and change in a global era*. London, Routledge.

Dean, J. (2002) *Publicity's secret*. Ithaca NY, Cornell University Press.

de Certeau, M. (1984) *The practice of everyday life*. Berkeley CA, University of California Press.

Deem, R. (2001) 'Globalisation, new managerialism, academic capitalism and entrepreneurialism in universities: is the local dimension still important?' *Comparative Education*, 37, 1, pp.7–20.

Deem, R. (2003) 'New managerialism, academic capitalism and entrepreneurialism', in Tight, M. (ed.) *Higher education reader*. London, Routledge (pp.287–302).

Deem, R. and Brehony, K. (2005) 'The case of new managerialism in higher education'. *Oxford Review of Education*, 31, 2, pp.213–231.

Deem, R., Hillyard, S. and Reed, M. (2007) *Knowledge, higher education, and the new managerialism: the changing management of UK universities*. London, Routledge.

Delgado, R. (1993) 'Rodrigo's sixth chronicle: intersections, essences, and the dilemma of social reform'. *New York University Law Review*, 68, pp.639–674.

Dubet, F. (2004) 'Dimensions and representations on student experience in mass university'. *Revue Francaise de Sociologie*, 35, 4, pp.511–532.

Dunleavy, P., Margetts, H., Bastow, S. and Tinkler, J. (2006) *Digital era governance: IT corporations, the state, and e-government*. Oxford, Oxford University Press.

Dutton, W. (2013) 'The social shaping of digital research'. *International Journal of Social Research Methodology*, 16, 3, pp.177–195.

Ellison, N., Steinfield, C. and Lampe, C. (2007) 'The benefits of Facebook "friends": social capital and college students' use of online social network sites'. *Journal of Computer-Mediated Communication*, 12, 4, pp.1143–1168.

Ernst and Young (2012) *University of the future: a thousand year old industry on the cusp of profound change*. Melbourne, Ernst & Young.

Esposito, A. (2013) 'Neither digital or open'. *First Monday*, 18, 1 (January), http://first-monday.org/ojs/index.php/fm/article/view/3881/3404.

Evans, C. (1979) *The mighty micro*. London, Coronet.

Eynon, R. (2005) 'The use of the internet in higher education'. *ASLIB Proceedings*, 57, 2, pp.168–180.

Fazackerley, A. (2013) 'Why are many academics on short-term contracts for years?' *The Guardian*, 4 February.

Feenberg, A. (1991) *Critical theory of technology*. Oxford, Oxford University Press.

Ferguson, L. (1977) *Historical archeology and the importance of material things*. Lansing MI, Society for Historical Archeology.

Ferguson, R. (2012) *The state of learning analytics in 2012: a review and future challenges*. Technical Report KMI-12-01, Milton Keynes, Knowledge Media Institute, Open University.

Ferlie, E., Musselin, C. and Andresani, G. (2009) 'The governance of higher education systems', in Paradeisie, C., Reale, E., Bleiklie, I. and Ferlie, E. (eds) *University governance*. Berlin, Springer (pp.1–19).

Francis, R. (2010) *The decentring of the traditional university*. London, Routledge.

Friedman, T. (2007) *The world is flat [release 3.0]*. New York, Farrar, Straus and Giroux.

Friesen, N. (2008) 'Critical theory: ideology critique and the myths of e-learning. *ACM Ubiquity*, 9, 22, http://ubiquity.acm.org/article.cfm?id=1386860.

Fuchs, C. (2008) *Internet and society: social theory in the information age*. London, Routledge.

Fuery, K. (2009) *New media: culture and image*. New York, Palgrave-Macmillan.

Fullick, M. (2012) 'The role of communication in governance: universities and (new) media'. *Journal of Professional Communication*, 2, 2, Article 3, http://digitalcommons.mcmaster.ca/jpc/vol2/iss2/3.

Fung, A. and Olin Wright, E. (2003) *Deepening democracy: institutional innovations in empowered participatory governance*. London, Verso.

Furlong, J. (2013) *Education – an anatomy of the discipline: rescuing the university project?* London, Routledge.

Gaffin, D. (1996) *In place*. Prospect Heights IL, Waveland Press.

Gallagher, S. and Garrett, G. (2013) *Disruptive education: technology-enabled universities*. Sydney, United States Study Centre and the New South Wales Government.

Gane, N. (2012) 'The governmentalities of neoliberalism: panopticism, post-panopticism and beyond'. *The Sociological Review*, 60, 4, pp.611–634.

Gell, M. and Cochrane, P. (1996) 'Learning and education in an information society', in Dutton, W. (ed.) *Information and communication technologies: visions and realities*. Oxford, Oxford University Press (pp.249–263).

Giddens, A. (2000) *Runaway world*. London, Routledge.

Gillberg, C. (2010) 'Review: Whose university is it, anyway? Power and privilege on gendered terrain'. *Gender and Education*, 22, 1, pp.132–134.

Gitlin, A. and Margonis, F. (1995) 'The political aspect of reform: teacher resistance as good sense'. *American Journal of Education*, 103, 3, pp.377–405.

Goffman, E. (1961) *Encounters: two studies in the sociology of interaction*. Indianapolis, Bobbs-Merrill.

Goodfellow, R. and Lea, M. (2013) 'Introduction: literacy, the digital and the university', in Goodfellow, R. and Lea, M. (eds) *Literacy in the digital university: critical perspectives on learning, scholarship and technology*. London, Routledge (pp.1–14).

Gorz, A. *(1982) A farewell to the working class*. London, Pluto.

Gourlay, L. (2014) 'Creating time: students, technologies and temporal practices in higher education'. *E-learning & Digital Media*, 11, 2 [forthcoming].

Gourlay, L. and Oliver, M. (2013) 'Beyond "the social": digital literacies as sociomaterial practice', in Goodfellow, R. and Lea, M. (eds) *Literacy in the digital university: critical perspectives on learning, scholarship and technology* London, Routledge (pp.79–94).

Gramsci, A. (1971/1929) *Selections from the prison notebooks*. London, Lawrence and Wishart.

Gregg, M. (2011) *Work's intimacy*. Cambridge, Polity.

Grieshaber, S. (2010) 'Beyond a battery hen model?' *British Journal of Sociology of Education*, 31, 4, pp.431–447.

Griffith, A. and André-Bechley, L. (2008) 'Institutional technologies: coordinating families and schools, bodies and texts', in Devault, M. (ed.) *People at work: life, power, and social inclusion in the new economy*. New York University Press (pp.40–56).

Gullifer, J. and Tyson, G. (2010) 'Exploring university students' perceptions of plagiarism: a focus group study'. *Studies in Higher Education*, 35, 4, pp.463–481.

Gullifer, J. and Tyson, G. (2014) 'Who has read the policy on plagiarism? Unpacking students' understanding of plagiarism'. *Studies in Higher Education* [forthcoming].

Gumport, P. (2007a) 'Reflections on a hybrid field', in Gumport, P. (ed.) *Sociology of higher education: contributions and their contexts*. Baltimore MA, John Hopkins University Press (pp.325–358).

Gumport, P. (2007b) 'Preface', in Gumport, P. (ed.) *Sociology of higher education: contributions and their contexts*. Baltimore MA, John Hopkins University Press (pp.vii–xii).

Gumport, P. (2007c) 'Sociology of higher education: an evolving field', in Gumport, P. (ed.) *Sociology of higher education: contributions and their contexts*. Baltimore MA, John Hopkins University Press (pp.17–51).

Haggis, T. (2006) 'Pedagogies for diversity: retaining critical challenge amidst fears of "dumbing down"'. *Studies in Higher Education*, 31, 5, pp.521–535.

Haigh, G. (2012) 'Brave news world: media is dead – long live media'. *Crikey*, 24 September, www.crikey.com.au/2012/09/24/brave-news-world-media-is-dead-long-live-media.

Harvey, D. (2005) *A brief history of neoliberalism*. Oxford, Oxford University Press.

Hassania, S. (2006) 'Locating digital divides at home, work, and everywhere else'. *Poetics*, 34, 4–5, pp.250–272.

Hatcher, R. (2000) 'Profit and power: business and Education Action Zones'. *Education Review*, 13, 1, pp.71–77.

Heath, C., Knoblauch, H. and Luff, P. (2000) 'Technology and social interaction: the emergence of workplace studies'. *British Journal of Sociology*, 51, 2, pp.299–320.

Hewitt, A., and Forte, A. (2006) 'Crossing boundaries: identity management and student/faculty relationships on the Facebook', paper presented at *Computer Supported Cooperative Work conference*, November, Banff.

Hil, R. (2012) *Whackademia: an insider's account of the troubled university*. Sydney, University of New South Wales Press.

Hilgers, M. (2010) 'The three anthropological approaches to neoliberalism'. *International Social Science Journal*, 61, pp.351–364.

Hillman, S. and Corkery, M. (2010) 'University infrastructural needs and decisions in moving towards online delivery programmes'. *Journal of Higher Education Policy and Management*, 32, 5, pp.467–474.

Hirschheim, R. (2005) 'Look before you leap'. *Communications of the ACM*, 48, 7, pp.97–101.

Hoffman, M. (2010) 'Disciplinary power', in Taylor, D. (ed.) *Michael Foucault*. Durham, Acumen (pp.27–39).

Holloway, J. (2002) *Change the world without taking power*. London, Pluto.

Hong, K., Ridzuan, A. and Kuek, M. (2003) 'Students' attitudes toward the use of the internet for learning: a study at a university in Malaysia'. *Educational Technology and Society*, 6, 2, pp.45–49.

Hurdley, R. (2010) 'The power of corridors: connecting doors, mobilizing materials, plotting openness'. *The Sociological Review*, 58, pp.45–64.

Jaffer, S. (2013) 'Spotted at university: crassness and cruelty'. *The Guardian*, 4 February, www.theguardian.com/education/2013/feb/04/spotted-at-university-misogyny-and-racism.

Jarvis, J. (2009) *What would Google do?* London, Collins.

Johnson, D. (2013) 'Technological change and professional control in the professoriate'. *Science, Technology & Human Values*, 38, 1, pp.126–149.

Joiner, R., Gavin, J., Brosnan, M., Crook, C., Duffield, J. et al. (2006) Internet identification and future internet use. *Cyberpsychology and Behavior*, 9, 4, pp.410–414.

Jones, C. (2012) 'Networked learning, stepping beyond the net generation and digital natives', in Dirckinck-Holmfeld, L., Hodgson, V. and McConnell, D. (eds) *Exploring the theory, pedagogy and practice of networked learning*. New York, Springer (pp.27–41).

Jones, C. (2013) 'The digital university: a concept in need of a definition', in Goodfellow, R. and Lea, M. (eds) *Literacy in the digital university: critical perspectives on learning, scholarship and technology*. London, Routledge (pp.162–172).

Jones, C. and Healing, G. (2010) 'Net generation students: agency and choice and the new technologies'. *Journal of Computer Assisted Learning*, 26, pp.344–356.

Jordan, T. (1999) *Cyberpower: the culture and politics of cyberspace and the internet*. London, Routledge.

Kellaway, L. (2013) 'I can't stop my cyber loafing'. *Financial Times*, 24 February, www.ft.com/cms/s/0/37a5b704-7b5d-11e2-8eed-00144feabdc0.html?.

Kennedy, G., Judd, T., Churchward, A. and Gray, K. (2008) 'First year students' experiences with technology: are they really digital natives?' *Australasian Journal of Educational Technology*, 24, 1, pp.108–122.

Kennedy, G., Judd, T., Dalgarno, B. and Waycott, J. (2010) 'Beyond natives and immigrants: exploring types of net generation students'. *Journal of Computer Assisted Learning*, 26, 5, pp.332–343.

Kenny, J., Fluck, A. and Jetson, T. (2012) 'Placing a value on academic work'. *Australian Universities' Review*, 54, 2, pp.50–60.

Kirkpatrick, G. (2005) 'Online "chat" facilities as pedagogic tools'. *Active Learning in Higher Education*, 6, 2, pp.145–159.

Kitto, S. and Higgins, V. (2003) 'Online university education: liberating the student?' *Science as Culture*, 12, 1, pp.23–58.

Klein, N. (2004) *The Vatican to Vegas*. New York, New Press.

Knight, P. (1995) *Assessment for learning in higher education*. London, Kogan Page.

Knox, D. (2010) 'Spies in the house of learning: a typology of surveillance in online learning environments', paper present to *EDGE 2010 – e-Learning: the horizon and beyond* conference, October, Newfoundland.

Krapp, P. (2011) *Noise channels: glitch and error in digital culture*. Minneapolis MN, University of Minnesota Press.

Kulik, J., Kulik, C. and Cohen, P. (1980) 'Effectiveness of computer-based college teaching: a meta-analysis of findings'. *Review of Educational Research*, 50, pp.525–544.

Law, J. (2004) *After method: mess in social science research*. London, Routledge.

Lehmann, W. (2013) 'In a class of their own: how working-class students experience university', in Brooks, R., McCormack, M. and Bhopal, K. (eds) *Contemporary debates in the sociology of education*. Basingstoke, Palgrave Macmillan (pp.93–111).

Little, B. (2002) 'UK institutional responses to undergraduates' term-time working'. *Higher Education*, 44, 3–4, pp.349–360.

Livingstone, S. (2009) *Children and the internet*. Cambridge, Polity.

Lovejoy, M. (2004) *Digital currents*. London, Routledge.

Lukes, S. (1974/2005) *Power: a radical view* (second edition). Basingstoke, Palgrave Macmillan.

McCabe, D. (2005) 'Cheating amongst college and university students: a North American perspective'. *International Journal of Educational Integrity*, 1, 1, http://ojs.ml.unisa. edu.au/index.php/IJEI/article/view/14.

MacFarlane, A. (1998) 'Information, knowledge and learning'. *Higher Education Quarterly*, 52, 1, pp.77–92.

McGowan, U. (2005) 'Educational integrity: a strategic approach to anti-plagiarism', paper presented to the Second Asia-Pacific Educational Integrity conference, University of Newcastle, December.

Mackenzie, A. (2010) *Wirelessness: radical empiricism in network cultures*. Cambridge MA, MIT Press.

McKenna, C. and Hughes, J. (2013) 'Values, digital texts and open practice', in Goodfellow, R. and Lea, M. (eds) *Literacy in the digital university: critical perspectives on learning, scholarship and technology*. London, Routledge (pp.15–26).

McKnight, J. (2012) 'A failure of Convivencia: democracy and discourse conflicts in a virtual government'. *Bulletin of Science Technology & Society*, 32, 5, pp.361–374.

McMillan, S. and Morrison, M. (2006) 'Coming of age with the internet: a qualitative exploration of how the internet has become an integral part of young people's lives'. *New Media and Society*, 8, 1, pp.73–95.

McNay, I. (2005) 'Higher education communities: divided they fail?' *Perspectives*, 9, 2, pp.39–44.

Mann, S. (2001) 'Alternative perspectives on the student experience'. *Studies in Higher Education*, 26, 1, pp.7–19.

Madden, M., Lenhart, A., Duggan, M., Cortesi, S. and Gasser, U. (2013) *Teens and technology 2013*. Washington DC, Pew Internet and American Life Project.

Madge, C., Meek, J., Wellens, J. and Hooley, T. (2009) 'Facebook, social integration and informal learning at university: it is more for socialising and talking to friends about work than for actually doing work'. *Learning, Media and Technology*, 34, 2, pp.141–155.

Maguire, M., Perryman, J., Ball, S. and Braun, A. (2011) 'The ordinary school: what is it?' *British Journal of Sociology of Education*, 32, 1, pp.1–16.

'Manifesto for teaching online' (2010) www.swop.education.ed.ac.uk/manifesto.html.

Maraizzi, C. (1994/2011) [trans. Mecchia, G.] *Capital and affects: the politics of the language economy*. Los Angeles CA, Semiotext(e).

Marginson, S. (2000) 'Rethinking academic work in the global era'. *Journal of Higher Education Policy and Management*, 22, 1, pp.23–35.

Marginson, S. (2013) 'The impossibility of capitalist markets in higher education'. *Journal of Education Policy*, 28, 3, pp.353–370.

Marvin, C. (1990) *When old technologies were new: thinking about electric communication in the late nineteenth century.* Oxford, Oxford University Press.

Massumi, B. (2002) *Parables of the virtual: movements, affect, sensation.* Durham NC, Duke University Press.

Masterman, E. and Shuyska, J. (2012) 'Digitally mastered? Technology and transition in the experience of taught postgraduate students'. *Learning, Media and Technology,* 37, 4, pp.335–354.

Mattern, S. (2007) 'Resonant texts: sounds of the American public library'. *Senses & Society,* 2, 3, pp.277–302.

Mattern, S. (2012) *Words in space,* www.wordsinspace.net/wordpresss.

Matthewman, S. (2011) *Technology and social theory.* London, Sage.

Mayer, A. and Puller, S. (2008) 'The old boy (and girl) network: social network formation on university campuses'. *Journal of Public Economics,* 92, 1–2, pp.329–347.

Means, A. (2011) 'Creativity as an educational problematic within the biopolitical economy', in Peters, M. and Bulut, E. (eds) *Cognitive capitalism, education and digital labor.* Berlin, Peter Lang (pp.211–228).

Menzies, H. (1998) 'Challenging capitalism in cyberspace', in McChesney, R., Wood, E. and Foster, J. (eds) *Capitalism and the information age.* New York, Monthly Review Press (pp.87–98).

Merton, R. (1957) 'The role-set: problems in sociological theory'. *British Journal of Sociology,* 8, pp.106–120.

Miron, G. and Urschel, J. (2012) *Understanding and improving full-time virtual schools: a study of student characteristics, school finance, and school performance in schools operated by K12 Inc.* Boulder CO, National Education Policy Center.

Mosco, V. (2004) *The digital sublime: myth, power and cyberspace.* Cambridge MA, MIT Press.

Munck, R. (2005) 'Neoliberalism and politics, and the politics of neoliberalism', in Saad-Filho, A. and Johnston, D. (eds) *Neoliberalism: a critical reader.* London, Pluto Press (pp.60–69).

Murphy, D. (2012) *The architecture of failure.* Winchester, Zero.

Murphy, M. (2009) 'Forms of rationality and public sector reform: Habermas, education and social policy', in Murphy, M and Fleming, T. (eds) *Habermas, critical theory and education.* London, Routledge (pp.78–94).

Nansen, B., Arnold, M., Gibbs, M. and Davis, H. (2011) 'Dwelling with media stuff: latencies and logics of materiality in four Australian homes'. *Environment and Planning D: Society and Space,* 29, pp.693–715.

Noam, E. (1995) 'Electronics and the dim future of the university'. *Science,* 270, 13, pp.247–249.

Noble, D. (1998) 'Digital diploma mills: the automation of higher education'. *First Monday,* 3, 1, http://firstmonday.org/ojs/index.php/fm/article/viewArticle/569/490.

Norton, L., Tilley, A., Newstead, S. and Franklyn-Stokes, A. (2001) 'The pressure of assessment in undergraduate courses and their effect on student behaviours'. *Assessment and Evaluation in Higher Education,* 26, 3, pp.269–284.

O'Toole, P. and Were, P. (2008) 'Observing places: using space and material culture in qualitative research'. *Qualitative Research,* 8, 5, pp.634–616.

Ong, A. (2007) *Neoliberalism as exception: mutations in citizenship and sovereignty.* Durham NC, Duke University Press.

Oxenham, M. (2013) *Higher education in liquid modernity.* London, Routledge.

Ozga, J. (2009) 'Governing education through data in England'. *Journal of Education Policy*, 24, 2, pp.149–162.

Ozler, L. (2012) 'Deakin University's Burwood Highway Frontage Building by Woods Bagot'. *Dexigner*, 12 March, www.dexigner.com/news/24745.

Pantzar, E. (2001) 'European perspectives on lifelong learning environments in the information society', in Karvonen, E. (ed.) *Informational societies*. Tampere, Tampere University Press (pp.240–258).

Paretta, L. and Catalano, A. (2013) 'What students really do in the library: an observational study'. *The Reference Librarian*, 54, 2, pp.157–167.

Parks, L. (2009) 'Around the antenna tree: the politics of infrastructural visibility'. *Flow*, 6 March, http://flowtv.org/2009/03/around-the-antenna-tree-the-politics-of-infrastructural-visibilitylisa-parks-uc-santa-barbara/.

Parr, C. (2012) 'Open University launches British MOOC platform to rival US providers'. *Times Higher Education Supplement*, 14 December.

Paulhus, D., Nathanson, C. and Williams, K. (2003) *A new look at the link between cognitive ability and exam cheating*. Vancouver BC, University of British Columbia.

Peters, M. (2011) *Neoliberalism and after: education, social policy and the crisis of Western capitalism*. Berlin, Peter Lang.

Pfeffer, T. (2012) *Virtualization of universities: digital media and the organization of higher education institutions*. Berlin, Springer.

Picciano, A. and Spring, J. (2013) *The great American education-industrial complex: ideology, technology and profit*. London, Routledge.

Popper, K. (1957/2002) *The poverty of historicism*. London, Routledge.

Poster, M. (1995) *The second media age*. Cambridge, Polity.

Prensky, M. (2003) *Digital natives*, www.marcprensky.com.

Prenksy, M. (2001) 'Digital natives, digital immigrants'. *On the Horizon*, 9, 5, pp.1–6.

Randall, D., Harper, R. and Rouncefield, M. (2007) *Fieldwork for design: theory and practice*. Berlin, Springer.

Rao, V. (2009) 'Embracing urbanism: the city as archive'. *New Literary History*, 40, 2, pp.371–383.

Readings, W. (1996) *The university in ruins*. Cambridge MA, Harvard University Press.

Rhoades, G. (2007) 'The study of the academic profession', in Gumport, P. (ed.) *Sociology of higher education: contributions and their contexts*. Baltimore MA, John Hopkins University Press (pp.113–145).

Richards, J. (2012) 'What has the internet ever done for employees? A review, map and research agenda'. *Employee Relations*, 34, 1, pp.22–43.

Rocco, E. and Warglien, M. (1995) *Computer mediated communication and the emergence of 'electronic opportunism'*. Department of Economics, Laboratory of Experimental Economics, University of Venice, Italy, http://eprints.biblio.unitn.it/archive/00000034/01/CEEL96_01.pdf.

Rowlands, I., Nicholas, D., Williams, P., Huntington, P., Fieldhouse, M. et al. (2008) 'The Google Generation: the information behavior of the researcher of the future'. *Aslib Proceedings*, 60, 4, pp.290–310.

Rybczynski, W. (1986) *Home: a short history of an idea*. New York, Viking.

Schlereth, T. (1982) *Material culture studies in America*. New York, Rowman Altamira.

Schuster, J. and Finkelstein, M. (2006) *American faculty: the restructuring of academic work and careers*. Baltimore, Johns Hopkins University Press.

Selwood, I. and Visscher, A. (2007) 'The potential of school information systems for enhancing school improvement', in Soguel, N. and Jaccard, P. (eds) *Governance and performance of education systems*. New York, Springer (pp.269–288).

Selwyn, N. (2009) 'Faceworking: exploring students' education-related use of Facebook'. *Learning, Media and Technology*, 34, 2, pp.157–174.

Sennett, R. (2012) *Together: the ritual, pleasures and politics of cooperation*. London, Allen Lane.

Shelton, C. (2014) 'Virtually mandatory: a survey of how discipline and institutional commitment shape university lecturers' perceptions of technology'. *British Journal of Educational Technology* [forthcoming].

Sinikara, K. (2013) 'Opening a new Helsinki University main library – a future vision, service design and collaboration'. *International Federation of Library Associations newsletter*, no. 1, pp.4–13.

Slaughter, S. and Leslie, G. (1997) *Academic capitalism*. Baltimore, John Hopkins University Press.

Smith, R. (2012) 'University futures'. *Journal of Philosophy of Education*, 46, 4, pp.649–662.

Smith, V. and Rhoades, G. (2006) 'Community college faculty and web-based classes'. *Thought and Action*, Fall 2006, pp.97–110, www.nea.org/assets/img/PubThoughtAndAction/TAA_06_10.pdf.

Snyder, B. (1971) *The hidden curriculum*. New York, Knopf.

Spigel, L. (1992) *Make room for TV: television and the family ideal in postwar America*. Chicago, University of Chicago Press.

Spring, J. (2012) *Education networks: power, wealth, cyberspace and the digital mind*. London, Routledge.

Standing, G. (2011) *The precariat: the new dangerous class*. London, Bloomsbury.

Suchman, L. (1987) *Plans and situated actions: the problem of human–machine communication*. Cambridge, Cambridge University Press.

Suppes, P. (1966) 'The uses of computers in education'. *Scientific American*, 215, pp.206–220.

Suspitsyna, T. (2010) 'Accountability in American education as a rhetoric and a technology of governmentality'. *Journal of Education Policy*, 25, 5, pp.567–586.

Swain, H. (2013) 'Are universities collecting too much information on staff and students?' *The Guardian*, 6 August, www.theguardian.com/education/2013/aug/05/electronic-data-trail-huddersfield-loughborough-university.

Szekeres, J. (2011) 'Professional staff carve out a new space'. *Journal of Higher Education Policy and Management*, 33, 6, pp.679–691.

Taylor, C. (2004) *Modern social imaginaries*. Durham NC, Duke University Press.

Tiffin, J. and Rajasingham, L. (1995) *In search of the virtual class: education in an information society*. London, Routledge.

Tindell, D. and Bohlander, R. (2012) 'The use and abuse of cell phones and text messaging in the classroom: a survey of college students'. *College Teaching*, 60, 1, pp.1–9.

Tronti, M. (2012) 'Our *operaismo*'. *New Left Review*, 73, January/February, http://newleftreview.org/II/73/mario-tronti-our-operaismo.

Tyack, D. and Tobin, W. (1995) 'The "grammar" of schooling: why has it been so hard to change?' *American Educational Research Journal*, 31, 3, pp.453–479.

Underwood, J. and Szabo, A. (2004) 'Cybercheats: is information and communication technology fuelling academic dishonesty?' *Active Learning in Higher Education*, 5, 2, pp.180–199.

Young, J. (2001) 'The cat-and-mouse game of plagiarism detection', *The Chronicle of Higher Education*, 6 July, http://chronicle.com/article/The-Cat-and-Mouse-Game-of/19463.

Wajcman, J. (2002) 'Addressing technological change: the challenge to social theory'. *Current Sociology*, 50, 3, pp.347–363.

Waks, L. (2012) 'Learning in the information age'. *Other Education: The Journal of Educational Alternatives*, 1, 1, pp.188–204.

Walker, J. (2010) 'Measuring plagiarism: researching what students do, not what they say they do'. *Studies in Higher Education*, 35, 1, pp.41–59.

Waring, T. and Skoumpopoulou, D. (2013) 'Emergent cultural change: unintended consequences of a Strategic Information Technology Services implementation in a United Kingdom university'. *Studies in Higher Education*, 38, 9, pp.1365–1381.

Weller, M. (2011) *The digital scholar: how technology is transforming scholarly practice.* London, Bloomsbury.

Williams, B. (2013) 'Control and the classroom in the digital university', in Goodfellow, R. and Lea, M. (eds) *Literacy in the digital university: critical perspectives on learning, scholarship and technology.* London, Routledge (pp.173–183).

Wilson, M. (2010) 'The impact of globalization on higher education: implications for globally networked learning environments'. *E–Learning and Digital Media*, 7, 2, pp.182–187.

Wilson, P. (2008) 'Jubilee Campus, Nottingham by Make'. *Architects Journal*, 2 October, www.architectsjournal.co.uk/jubilee-campus-nottingham-by-make/1885933.article.

Winner, L. (1998) 'Report from the Digital Diploma Mills conference'. *Science as Culture*, 7, 3, pp.369–377.

Wolff, J. (2013) 'It's too early to write off the lecture'. *The Guardian*, 25 June, www.theguardian.com/education/2013/jun/24/university-lecture-still-best-learning.

Wolfson, L. (2013) 'Venture capital needed for "broken" US education, Thrun says'. *Bloomberg Businessweek*, 18 June, www.businessweek.com/news/2013-06-18/venture-capital-needed-for-broken-u-dot-s-dot-education-thrun-says.

Woods Bagot Architects (2012) *Deakin University Melbourne, Australia: Building*, www.e-architect.co.uk/melbourne/deakin_university_building.htm.

Woolgar, S. (2002) 'Five rules of virtuality', in Woolgar, S. (ed.) *Virtual society? Technology, cyberbole, reality.* Oxford, Oxford University Press (pp.1–22).

Wright, W., Knight, P. and Pomerleau, N. (1999) 'Portfolio people: teaching and learning dossiers and the future of higher education'. *Innovative Higher Education*, 24, 2, pp.89–102.

Wynne, B. (1996) 'May the sheep safely graze? A reflexive view of the expert–lay knowledge divide', in Lash, S., Szerszynski, B. and Wynne, B. (eds) *Risk, environment and modernity: towards a new ecology.* London, Sage (pp.44–83).

Index